D0338570

Social
Responsibility
in Marketing

Social Responsibility in Marketing

A PROACTIVE AND PROFITABLE MARKETING MANAGEMENT STRATEGY

A. Coskun Samli

Quorum Books
Westport, Connecticut • London

Library of Congress Cataloging-in-Publication Data

Samli, A. Coskun.
    Social responsibility in marketing : a proactive and profitable
marketing management strategy / A. Coskun Samli.
        p.   cm.
    Includes bibliographical references and index.
    ISBN 0-89930-628-4 (alk. paper)
    1. Marketing—Management.   2. Marketing—Social aspects.   3. Green
marketing—Management.   4. Social responsibility of business.
I. Title.
HF5415.13.S24   1992
658.8'02—dc20   92-9810

British Library Cataloguing in Publication Data is available.

Library of Congress Catalog Card Number: 92-9810
ISBN: 0-89930-628-4

First published in 1992

Quorum Books, 88 Post Road West, Westport, CT 06881
An imprint of Greenwood Publishing Group, Inc.

Printed in the United States of America

The paper used in this book complies with the
Permanent Paper Standard issued by the National
Information Standards Organization (Z39.48-1984).

10 9 8 7 6 5 4 3 2 1

This book is dedicated to ambitious marketing decision makers everywhere, who would want a very positive profit picture but who also *care*.

Contents

| *Exhibits*

| Preface

It is my hope that this controversial book will raise many issues and be instrumental in the emergence of numerous decisions, debates, and, above all, socially responsible marketing decisions that will benefit society as a whole.

It is high time to realize that every time a marketing decision takes place at the microlevel, it has far-reaching societal implications at the macrolevel. It is not quite correct that as an individual firm pursues big returns and very satisfactory profits, the society also will benefit. Unless the micro and macro conditions are coordinated, the society may be hurt rather than rewarded.

This book reemphasizes the known fact that the market is not perfect. In fact, it is far from it and is getting worse. Hence, unless conscious and proactive actions take place to benefit both the firm and the market simultaneously, decisions and behavior of individual firms could be detrimental to the society.

This book takes the position that what is beneficial to the market could be quite beneficial to some or all in the market (both firms and consumers). However, what might be beneficial to a firm does not have to be beneficial to anybody but that firm alone; this is particularly true in the case of oligopolies and mainly true for monopolies.

The general theme of this book is illustrated in Exhibit P-1. As seen in the exhibit, marketing decisions that will benefit society will improve the quality of life (QOL) for the consumers. This situation

Exhibit P-1
Contribution of Socially Responsible
Marketing

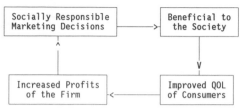

also will improve the profit picture of the firm simultaneously. Thus, marketing is not only a powerful social process but, if used effectively, it is an enhancer of the QOL. Effective use of marketing in this book is construed to be socially responsible marketing.

The book begins with a brief introduction displaying the two extreme views about the market. It proposes that the market is not sacrosanct and, if left alone, it does not function in an all-beneficial and corrective manner.

Chapter 1 sets the tone of the book by exploring what social responsibility is and the relationship between the individual and the society.

Chapter 2 explores earlier works and thinking regarding marketing's social responsibilities. It identifies some major problems in the prevailing American markets.

Chapter 3 sets forth four types of marketing: negative, inactive, reactive, and proactive. It posits that proactive marketing is a must for socially responsible behavior.

Chapter 4 establishes the fact that a large proportion of Americans are not "equal opportunity consumers." Indeed, equal opportunity for American consumers is simply a myth.

Chapter 5 points out that in addition to not having equal opportunity consumers, American society has large numbers of vulnerable consumers. These are the poor, uneducated, and less-competent consumers. These people need to be protected by laws, consumer education, and consumer information.

Chapter 6 deals with the issue of ethics. It proposes that ethics and pursuant ethical behavior do not exist or do not work well.

Chapter 7 delves into some key issues of questionable marketing that worsen already questionable overall market behavior.

Chapter 8 examines just what constitutes consumer-friendly products. It puts forth a model to develop such products.

Chapter 9 makes a case for much-needed consumer-friendly services. It presents a model for developing consumer-friendly bank services as an example.

Chapter 10 touches upon a very critical topic of environment-friendly products. The environment must be suitable for the society to achieve a higher quality of life.

Chapter 11 distinguishes between the two democracies: political and economic. It posits that these two democracies should check and balance each other. When they do, they enhance competition and improve consumer well-being.

Chapter 12 analyzes the difference between marketing efficiency and marketing effectiveness. The two must coexist for the best societal results.

Finally, the epilogue puts forth a research agenda to improve marketing's performance in the society and make it more productive.

Many people have contributed directly and indirectly to the development of this book. Early on, my thinking was formed by marketing theory and welfare economics courses I took at Michigan State University in East Lansing. Over the years, my discussions with my friend and mentor, Stan Hollander, (even though he may not agree with many positions I take in this book) further formed my thinking.

My friend, colleague, and coauthor of many years, Professor Joe Sirgy, always has been available to argue or interact. His influence on my thinking has been profound.

My colleagues and coauthors in certain chapters in this book, William Wilkinson, Mary Ann Lederhaus, and Cheryl Frohlich, made particular contributions to my thinking. Finally, my friend and colleague, Steve Paulson, has read and critiqued some of the chapters and made valuable suggestions. This book could not have been written without the research help I received from my research assistants, David McDonald and Riaz M. Abdul. Perhaps most of all, our secretaries, Jane Wood and Betty Geitz, always were there to help. But nobody's contribution has been as great as that of my secretary, Leanna Payne, who not only typed from my hardly legible handwritten notes, but also painstakingly read every chapter and gave me her seal of approval, which I value very highly. Over the years, thousands of my students argued, interacted, and perhaps, at times, were forced to listen to my rather unusual ideas. I benefitted from these experiences. Finally, Beverly Chapman gave me a helping hand in editing the book. To these and many other people who over the years discussed, interacted, or researched these issues with me, I extend my deep gratitude. I, however, am solely responsible for the contents of this book. I certainly hope that it makes a modest contribution to the well-being of not a few but *all*.

Social
Responsibility
in Marketing

| *Introduction*

In order to introduce this book properly, it is necessary to point out two totally opposing points of view and then take a position.

John F. Gaski (1985) stated that:

> The "societal marketing" concept, or the view that marketing has a greater social responsibility than just satisfying customers at a profit, is an erroneous and counterproductive idea. For Marketers to attempt to serve the best interests of society is not only undemocratic but dangerous as well.

When he wrote these lines, John Gaski made many key assumptions. First, he assumed that customers are very knowledgeable and therefore they can make very good purchase decisions. Thus, they all are satisfied as consumers living in our market system. This would be correct only under perfect competition assumptions. Today's consumer probably knows much less (relatively speaking) than those in Adam Smith's times. This is despite the fact that today's consumer may be better educated. Today's consumer environment is so much more confusing that the need for information in order for the modern consumer to make optimal decisions is acute. Moreover, consumer choices are so much greater that consumers actually are further away from making good decisions than were their ancestors.

Gaski discusses the undemocratic nature of marketers' use of a social responsibility path. This is a very curious position to take.

Democracy can be improved only when the constituencies are well informed and they are able to choose from a good group of candidates or they make a choice of a number of well-thought-out issues. Thus, if consumers are well informed and making decisions to purchase a series of good products or services, it becomes obvious that their choice (or vote) becomes more meaningful in terms of improving the quality of life (QOL) in that society for those consumers.

Finally, Gaski's statement about a socially responsible behavior path is dangerous. He maintains that marketing is not in a position to make socially responsible decisions because it does not know enough about it. However, one may ask who other than a particular business knows more about its particular products or services? How could Rely tampon users or the Bon Vivant soup consumers have known that they would die if they used these products? How could the average consumer know that Red Dye No. 2 would cause cancer? Questions of this kind could go on and on. The business is much closer to the scientific, societal, and consumer-related aspects of its products and services. The same business easily could satisfy (not pacify) the consumer by providing a product that not only is usable and acceptable but also safe for the individual, safe for the environment, and good for the diminishing resources of our society. What if it really would not take much extra resources and money to develop such products and services? Who would benefit? What if our society really were to get ahead because sound and safe products and services were distributed effectively among informed and protected constituencies? And what if this is done without any discrimination in the marketplace? What would be the outcome to business? Would society's gains be too great a sacrifice for business?

This book maintains that society's well-being and business' well-being are one and the same. If the society becomes progressively worse off, the business sector cannot survive. Marketing plays a significant role in achieving such a well-being in the society by providing better QOL to all in that society, not only to a privileged few.

There are other assumptions that are made by Gaski that particularly need to be examined. Among these, the most important one is that the market is borderline perfect (if not totally perfect) and, left alone, it will take care of all of society's problems. Perhaps William

M. Dugger's (1989) position will respond to this position. He states that:

The simple observation that the market is an instituted process rather than a natural equilibrium takes on great significance because it makes accountable men and women who exercise power behind the protection of the market myth. That simple observation eliminates their protection. When the market is understood as an instituted process, those who institute it can be held responsible.

Behind the Gaski position is the myth that the market is not only natural, but is almost sacrosanct. By not interfering with it and by letting it function without outside interference, the market will yield the best results. But Dugger points out that the "enabling myths" that enable the upper strata to maintain dominance over the lower are a myth. He maintains that those who benefit from the institutionalized status quo believe that they benefit because their personal gifts or efforts merit it. He further points out that those who are for the status quo and the natural balance of the market ignore two simple facts: (1) people are educable, and (2) many people do not have equal opportunity.

This book posits that consumers are educable and must have equal opportunity. Unlike the thinking of the market as a "product of divine dispensation" (Dugger, 1989, 614), it is maintained here that if the market is improved through socially responsible marketing behavior, not only those who are in power will retain their power, but others will be better off as well. This is termed *enlightened self-interest*. If the market improves in its overall performance, the QOL in the society will be enhanced. However, if the society becomes more and more disjointed in that there are widening discrepancies between "haves" and "have-nots," it is doubtful that those who are in better positions can maintain their relative status. If the discrepancy between haves and have-nots is widening, in a democracy haves may find themselves in a difficult position. But, above all, if the society does not survive, the market cannot survive, and marketing itself becomes a myth.

Thus, in this book it is maintained that marketing decision makers are obligated to take actions that also protect and enhance society's interests (Davis 1975). This proactive behavior will improve the profit picture for marketing and business decision makers as it improves the well-being of consumers as a whole.

Since the currently prevailing market cannot provide the mythical outcomes that classical and neoclassical economists have proposed, it is necessary to take a socially responsible behavior pattern and be proactive in its implementation. Thus, we take Dugger's position about the market's not being sacrosanct. The crux of the general message in this book is that consumers' well-being without discrimination through genuine and effective competition is the goal for marketing. This goal can be achieved and must be achieved so that we all can enjoy a better quality of life.

REFERENCES

Davis, Keith. 1975. "Five Propositions for Social Responsibility." *Business Horizons* (June):19–24.

Dugger, William M. 1989. "Instituted Process and Enabling Myth: The Two Faces of the Market." *Journal of Economic Issues* (June):607–615.

Gaski, John F. 1985. "Dangerous Territory: The Societal Marketing Concept Revisited." *Business Horizons* (July/August):42–47.

1 | Socially Responsible Marketing Is Good Marketing

It may come as a surprise to some and it may make other skeptics smile, but I believe social responsibility in marketing is good marketing. We are dealing with a profession that provided the society with Salk vaccine as well as Tender Vittles. If the society expresses its needs and desires clearly, and if marketing can be more productive in developing more socially responsible goods and services, the whole society will be better off.

Marketing provides goods and services for the society. It also makes a significant impact on the variety and choice that are made available and the purchase process that ultimately determines the society's quality of life (QOL). It is obvious that marketing plays a very critical role in the well-being of the society. In any society, any force that has a lot of power certainly has much responsibility as well. In other words, marketing with all its acclaimed or not-so-acclaimed power, should and does have some very serious social responsibilities.

Just what is social responsibility? *The New Webster's Dictionary* (1986) defines *responsibility* as duty and accountability. What are marketing's duties and accountabilities and from where do these stem? These are the key questions to be addressed in this chapter.

MARKETING'S DUTY AND ACCOUNTABILITY

Marketing is a process that generates exchange among people, among institutions, and among people and institutions. As this exchange process takes place, marketing generates and delivers QOL. Thus, it is obvious that marketing has a very important role to play in the society. It would be reasonable to raise the question: Should marketing consider that it has certain duties and accountabilities, or would these be taken care of in a freely functioning market?

It has been more than 200 years since Adam Smith (1779) articulated a freely functioning market and perfect competition. Of course, Adam Smith lived and functioned in a uniquely different environment. He saw many enterprising, very small businesses that, left alone, would function very sensibly (or rationally) to enhance their effectiveness. Entrepreneurs who ran these businesses were shrewd enough to know all that was needed for their businesses and they functioned accordingly. He also had faith in human beings who, left alone, could make simple but good decisions for their own benefit. Leaving the people and businesses alone implied the existence of *invisible hands*. These are natural forces to keep the economy stable and in full-employment status.

How Invisible Are the Invisible Hands?

If we consider the description of the market and conditions assumed and discussed in classical economics, it is reasonable to conclude that the market takes care of itself. If marketing does not do the job right, the invisible hand would take care of the situation by perhaps penalizing marketing or forcing it to perform in a different way. However, the unique concept of invisible hands basically implies that the market functions almost perfectly and to the utmost satisfaction of consumers. Thus, if there are irregularities or dissatisfactions related to marketing, they are expected to be resolved all by themselves.

This particular concept almost implies that not only may there be no need for social responsibility considerations for marketing, but there may not even be a need for marketing.

If we compare Adam Smith's market with the current American market, the picture becomes rather clear that the two have basically nothing in common and, therefore, what might have held true in Adam Smith's market is not likely to hold true in the present-day American market. Exhibit 1-1 illustrates this contrast.

The exhibit compares six basic criteria relating to Adam Smith's

Exhibit 1-1

A Comparison of Adam Smith's Market to Current American Market

	Adam Smith's Market	Current American Market
Enterprises	Numerous and very small	Relatively fewer and many are too big
Business Decision Areas	Rather simple, dealing with some basic decisions	Multitudinous, complex and dealing with multiple decisions
Information	Limited but fully available both to business and individuals	Tremendously voluminous and not quite available to all businesses or all people
Consumers	Almost fully aware of their rather simple needs	Multiple choice options and less aware of complex needs
Entrance of Enterprises	Very easy, no hindrances	In some industries it is almost impossible
Pricing Power	All are price takers	Most are price makers

market as well as the American market: (1) enterprises; (2) business decisions; (3) information; (4) consumers; (5) entering the market; and (6) pricing power.

Enterprises

Enterprises in Adam Smith's market were very small and numerous. No one firm could make an impact on the market. They could enter or exit freely. They also were very competitive.

Unlike the classical conditions, in today's market at the threshold of the 21st century there is a tendency for oligopolies to emerge. Small businesses are not as small as those that existed in Adam Smith's times, and large businesses are incredibly large. None of these existed in Adam Smith's times.

Business Decisions

Business decisions in Adam Smith's time were simple and, because of competition, not much different from certain norms, which are followed by all businesses. Thus, because of simplicity and competition, businesses made simple and rational decisions.

Business decisions in the modern American market are multidimensional, extremely complex, and extremely numerous. It is impossible to assume that business decisions even approach rationality, let alone perfect rationality. Modern American businesses have to make very complex decisions and, because of the multidimensionality of their decision conditions, they make many decisions. Thinking that all of these decisions can be rational, leading to optimalities, is quite unrealistic.

Consumers

Consumers in Adam Smith's market were aware of their needs and what they must acquire to satisfy those needs. Because of their closeness to small business units and because of the limited nature of their choices, they were able to make simple but very positive decisions.

Today's consumer has a tremendous number of choices. Most of the products are complex and many food products have additives, preservatives, and other chemicals. Some of them are dangerous. Many of them have hazardous long-term effects. Many household chemicals are poisonous and environmentally offensive. It is virtually impossible for the modern consumer to be rational and utility maximizing. Normal average consumers typically are confused and have difficulty making satisfactory decisions. Even though they may have the capability to evaluate functional product attributes in a rational manner, they lack the time and motivation to do so (Kassarjian 1986; Engel, Blackwell, and Miniard 1990).

Information

Information in Adam Smith's market was simple and available. Neither consumers nor businesses needed access to huge databases to make reasonable and rational decisions. Simplicity of the community and the market conditions enabled both businesses and consumers to develop access to equally simple information for their decision processes.

In the modern American market, just like all the complicated factors interacting with the market or influencing it, information also is complex. Information's complexity is due to two factors. First, it is extremely voluminous; there is an information explosion that has been going on for decades. Second, there are many different media disseminating this information in the marketplace. Much of this complex information is needed by consumers as well as businesses to make decisions. Information is neither readily available nor easily accessible. This is the other end of the equation, and causes irrationality of consumers and businesses. These two groups cannot possibly make rational decisions when information is not readily available or easily accessible.

Entering the Market

Entry in Adam Smith's market was very easy. New businesses entered the market without any interferences. Many small businesses that were quite similar to each other managed to enter and survive in the market. Again, because of simplicity of the market and proximity to consumers, these little businesses managed to serve the market well and survive.

On the other hand, in modern America the market is not only very complex, but it also is not quite open for entry. Today's market has many barriers to entry. Some of these are economic and others are legal.

Economic barriers are related to unevenness of economic power distribution. In a number of major industries, the market can be described as oligopolistic. In such cases, the oligopolists are so powerful and the entry requirements, in terms of capital, know-how, and other similar resources, are so outrageous that new firms hardly can enter the market. In such other industries as some of the consumer services, entry is rather easy, but survival is extremely difficult.

Legal barriers are related to local or federal regulations. In many industries such as banking, insurance, or health-related activities, there are very strict local and federal regulations restricting entry that are being enforced vigorously.

Pricing Power

Pricing power of enterprises in Adam Smith's times were such that firms were perfectly competitive. With such a competitive picture comes the status of being a price taker. The term *price taker* means that nobody has certain monopoly power to manipulate prices. All participants followed a market-determined pricing policy. However, in modern times many businesses have taken the position of being price makers. As monopolists or at least as monopolistic competitors, they assume the role of being price makers. They have more independence and a lot more power than their counterparts in Adam Smith's times.

As seen in Exhibit 1-1 and the discussion above, the invisible hands of Adam Smith's classical economic theory are no longer in existence. Since the conditions are not present for the microeconomic activities leading to a macroeconomic optimality, it is unrealistic to expect the presence of perfect competition in the contemporary American market.

The Results of the Absent Invisible Hands

The perfect competition and its implications in Adam Smith's times would lead one to believe that, unchecked, the market conditions are so appropriate that the economy takes care of itself and the people who are participating in it. This would mean that the economic well-being of the consumer and the society both are taken care of and approaching certain optimality.

If these conditions are prevalent and these outcomes are acknowledged, then there is no reason for social responsibility considerations. The firms that do not act responsibly will be boycotted by consumers and will be eliminated. Thus, the firm's dutiful and accountable behavior is related to its economic performance, and the market takes care of the efficient and effective as it eliminates the inefficient and ineffective.

However, as we establish that the conditions that prevailed in Adam Smith's market leading to perfect competition are no longer present, we must discard the invisible hands. Invisible hands in Adam Smith's time were construed to be certain natural forces that invariably adjusted the market conditions for the better. They eliminated the inefficient or provided better utilization of resources, or created more competition if there were extraordinary profits in an industry.

In today's market, we still can assume that there may be some semblance of invisible hands. But, if they do function, there is no reason to assume that they will function in a positive manner. Because of the lack of information and unevenness of economic power, invisible hands may cause further accumulation of economic power or misallocation of resources, among other malfunctions.

The reason for malfunctions in the present market is that the necessary conditions for perfect competition are not present as they might have been in Adam Smith's market. Thus, there is no reason to assume that at both the micro- and macrolevels economic and marketing functions will lead to satisfactory results and the market, if uninterrupted, will take care of everything. The lack of perfect competition and Adam Smith's invisible hands, by definition, implies the possibility of the presence of many malfunctions in the market and the economy. These malfunctions or less-than-optimal results are furthered by irresponsible behavior on the part of businesses. Part of the irresponsible behavior causing less than optimalities—in fact, unsatisfactory economic results—is related to marketing. Social responsibility in marketing, therefore, would be, indeed should be, geared toward achieving those results that would have been achieved if competition was perfect and the invisible hands truly were functional. Without certain socially responsible behavior by the overall marketing process in the society, there is no possibility of optimizing the economic performance of the society and providing optimum QOL for the society.

SOCIAL RESPONSIBILITY IN MARKETING

The marketing process facilitates distribution and exchange of goods and services in a society. Subsequently, this process provides a certain QOL for the whole society. In all of these three phases of the overall marketing process (i.e., distribution, exchange of goods and services, and generation of the QOL), there are alternatives. In a very general sense, the two alternatives are (1) marketing to individuals or specific groups, and (2) marketing to the whole society and within that society. While marketing to individuals or specific (privileged) groups may emphasize the advancement of their well-beings, marketing to the whole society would imply enhancement of the society's QOL as a whole.

If the society's well-being is enhanced, everybody's QOL will improve accordingly. If, on the other hand, marketing enhances the well-being of a select few, the remainder of the society could be shortchanged. Since marketing is a process, even though a very powerful one, it can go either way. It can be used to enhance the well-being of only a select few or to enhance the well-being of the whole society. Assuming the second choice is better than the first, it is necessary to determine how marketing can be used to enhance the well-being of the whole society. It is posited in this book that social responsibility issues, if handled properly, will set marketing on the right course toward improving the existing QOL of the society and hence improving all individuals' well-being as well.

Failure to establish a marketing system that will yield the same results as Adam Smith's invisible hands would imply marketing to a privileged few. This means that in the name of individualism a few individuals' well-being is considered more important than the well-being of the rest of the whole society. Furthermore, the failure to establish social responsibility in marketing is likely to lead to what, some years ago, Samli and Sirgy (1982) termed *marketing pathology*.

Marketing Pathology

Although some discussion of marketing as a living system is presented below in different sections of this book (see, for instance, Chapters 2 and 3), it is necessary to articulate two points here as regards marketing pathology.

First, a successful system's approach to marketing has to have certain characteristics, which are very similar to those of living systems (Alderson 1957, 1965). Such a system has its birth, growth, propagation, decline, and death (Miller 1978). Marketing, just as other living systems, must demonstrate prolonged periods of steady state. This is an equilibrium condition in which the opposing variables are in balance. All living systems are motivated to maintain such a homeostatic state and, therefore, maintain an orderly balance among its subsystems that process matter, energy, and information (Miller 1978). If such a steady state is not attained over a prolonged period of time, the system starts to show pathological symptoms and develops pathological conditions that may not be reversible naturally.

Second, if marketing as a system within itself and a subsystem within the society does not perform well, it presents, in essence, what may be called marketing pathology (Samli and Sirgy 1982).

It is maintained throughout this book that Adam Smith's market, leading to perfect competition and a steady state, has given way to the modern market conditions. These conditions started yielding a less-than-perfect competition, and are further and further away from Adam Smith's original conditions. As these conditions changed, the general course of the economy changed also. The change from perfect competition to substantially less-than-perfect competition first eliminated the necessary steadiness of the system. This lack of steadiness generated the conditions that are not likely to reverse themselves and return to Adam Smith's conditions. Second, the change from perfect competition to current-day market conditions created marketing pathology characteristics. Marketing pathology characteristics, by definition, require social responsibility functions to rectify themselves, otherwise, the society may reach a course of self-destruction.

Causes of Marketing Pathology

In order to cope with marketing pathology, it is necessary to understand and eliminate pathological causes. Similarly, social responsibility at least may pacify the pathological implications or the impact. It is not only improbable, but totally impossible, to go back to Adam Smith's market. Therefore, by definition, we must use the social responsibility alternative. Just what causes marketing pathology? What are the typical outcomes of this pathology? How are these pathological causes related to Adam Smith's conditions? Exhibit 1-2 provides answers to these particular questions.

There are at least six major causes of marketing pathology (Samli and Sirgy 1982).

1. Inadequate levels of raw material, energy, and other resource inputs
2. Inappropriate forms of raw material, energy inputs, and other resources
3. Inadequate levels of marketing information inputs
4. Overall maladaptive marketing philosophy
5. Abnormalities in internal product-related processes
6. Abnormalities in internal marketing information processes

Exhibit 1-2
Marketing Pathology, Outcomes, and Adam Smith's Market Interpretation

Pathological Causes	Marketing Outcomes	In Adam Smith's Terminology
Inadequate inputs	Dangerous products; wasteful or dysfunctional products	Less than optimization; irrational behavior
Inappropriate forms of inputs	Dangerous short-run and long run biological and genetic impacts; poor environmental impact	Inefficient production processes; irrational behavior
Inadequate market information	Mismatch of supply and demand; waste of resources; dysfunctional products	Less than perfect knowledge
Maladaptive marketing philosophy	Mismatch of supply and demand; waste of resources	Less than perfect knowledge and irrational behavior
Abnormal internal product processes	Waste of resources; dangerous and dysfunctional products	Inefficient behavior; irrational behavior
Abnormal internal marketing information	Wrong product prioritization; misallocation of the firm's resources	Less than perfect knowledge; inefficient behavior

Inadequate Levels of Raw Material, Energy, and Other Resource Inputs

Insufficient raw materials and energy resources, utilized in production and distribution, may produce less-than-satisfactory goods and services or a shortage of goods and services. Furthermore, the products could be dangerous, wasteful, or dysfunctional.

Less-than-adequate levels of raw materials have caused a shortening of the product life, which may be detected in such products as soaps, shoes, light bulbs, and wristwatches. By using less than adequate inputs, American auto tire manufacturers produced a dangerous product that forced Ralph Nader to wage war against the manufacturers (Nader 1957).

Inappropriate Forms of Raw Material, Energy Inputs, and Other Resources

Utilizing inputs that should not be used, be it Red Dye No. 2, saccharine, benzine in Perrier, or poison in Bon Vivant soups, is likely to cause not only consumer dissatisfaction, but rather serious health hazards. Items ranging from lead in the drinking water to mercury in dental fillings are being criticized as being extremely dangerous. There are no doubts about the dangers of asbestos or Agent Orange. This list could go on and on. Many of these substances are major inputs in many different products and cause life-threatening diseases; they illustrate inappropriate inputs leading to severe health hazards. These situations cause further marketing pathology, perhaps in terms of causing failure for the company (e.g., negative image, mounting political pressures, product recalls, illnesses in epidemic proportions, etc.). All in all, these situations may be endangering the balance of the total social system by creating health hazards or environmental threats.

Inadequate Levels of Marketing Information Inputs

Inadequate information is likely to cause the production and delivery of unneeded goods, low-quality goods, unnecessary goods, or goods that are potentially harmful to either the individual consumer or the society at large. Marketing myopia, posited by Levitt (1960, 1975), is a direct result of less-than-adequate information concerning the potential short-range and long-range merits and ill effects of marketing goods and services. Proctor and Gamble certainly had less-than-adequate information when it introduced Rely tampons. Ford Motor Company had inadequate information about Pinto's back side being explosive, which eventually caused hundreds of fatal accidents. Similarly, makers of the Audi 5000 did not have proper information about the car's going backward in special circumstances, again causing fatal accidents and very extensive damage to the company's profit picture. Ford Motor Company had inadequate information that caused failure to market Edsel successfully (Hartley 1986). Similarly, DuPont discontinued Corfam because it had inadequate knowledge about the product's limitations.

Overall Maladaptive Marketing Philosophy

Maladaptive marketing philosophy refers to a deficient or defective corporate philosophy concerning the organizational inability to respond to external and higher needs prevailing in the society. An example of a defective corporate philosophy is one that reflects marketing executives' beliefs that their primary and sole responsibility lies only with the stockholders. They think that the primary and, indeed, the only goal is profit making. Thus, such other considerations as helping the surrounding communities, helping combat pollution and other ecological problems, and helping to enhance the society's QOL all are outside the realm of their marketing responsibilities. They consider these activities to be altruistic and charitable, having nothing to do with the business and economic considerations.

Maladaptive marketing philosophy cannot make the necessary changes to adapt to external changes and unexpected economic conditions. This philosophy leads to a mismatch between supply and demand and therefore leads to waste of resources as well as the production of dangerous and ineffective products.

An *adaptive marketing philosophy* is one which admits that the marketing organization not only is responsible to its stockholders but also to the society at large. It is responsible to contribute to the enhancement of the society from which it receives permission to use the resources, to exploit opportunities, and dump its garbage.

Abnormalities in Internal Product-Related Processes

Abnormalities in internal matter- and energy-related processes refer to malfunctioning problems in manufacturing and in assembling the final product. It also can refer to poor or inferior machinery and matter-energy systems used in developing the product. All of these lead to inferior, dysfunctional, and perhaps dangerous products. One wonders why in recent years the performance of the Japanese auto industry has appeared to have far exceeded the American auto industry. This observation is attributed to the constantly increasing share of Japanese cars in the total American auto market. The key factor causing this situation is the internal matter-energy processes in the auto industry. The American auto industry has not been improving its productive capabilities by using improved matter-energy processes. As the overall technology advances, those productive facilities that are not keeping up with these advances eventually develop abnormalities in internal matter-energy processes.

These abnormalities will cause a mismatch between supply and demand. They lead to a substantial waste of resources. Furthermore, they may cause dysfunctional products.

Abnormalities in the Internal Marketing Information Processes

Even though information may exist at a satisfactory level in proper format and quality, if marketing organizations do not process and use this information effectively, it serves no purpose. In such cases, the company may develop wrong product prioritization and produce wrong products. As a result, misallocation of the firm's resources may set in. This situation may cause unnecessary waste of scarce resources in addition to the possibility of the firm's failure.

For instance, it is possible that all the salespeople realize that the newly introduced large car does not have a market demand because it does not meet the market specifications, but this information is not sought out by the management of the auto manufacturing firm. As a result, abnormalities in internal information process set in that, in turn, lead to marketing pathology. Any time the information is processed improperly or totally ignored, it is likely that a pathological situation will occur.

SOCIAL RESPONSIBILITY: THE TASK AHEAD

It is maintained in this chapter that all managerial marketing decisions have social implications. Unless corporate marketing decisions are made within the constraints of the greater system, the consequences can be detrimental. If, on the other hand, the marketing decision makers can respond to the six conditions of marketing pathology and eliminate the causes of pathology or malfunctioning in the system, the total marketing system as well as individual firms can survive and prosper.

If any or all of these conditions are acutely and/or chronically violated, then there is reasonable doubt that the whole socioeconomic system could function harmoniously. Thus, the true social responsibility of marketing emerges. Unless enlightened self-interest guides marketing away from special individuals or groups to the whole system to function effectively and closer to Adam Smith's market, the society is likely to show pathological symptoms. If marketing eliminates the six pathological causes and acts socially responsibly, there will be no end to growth and progress in the society and to enhancement of QOL.

Social responsibility of marketing, therefore, should not be considered a passing fancy or some idealistic scheme. Not only is it here to stay, but failure of marketing as a discipline and as a social process to take its social responsibility seriously can be detrimental not only to society at large, but also to marketing itself. Marketing is part of a broader system, a suprasystem. If marketing is to survive in the context of a free-enterprise environment, with no invisible hands in Adam Smith's sense, it has to adjust to the strains and stresses stemming from deviating from Adam Smith's market. This deviation is causing pathological conditions within the marketing system as well as in its environment. As part of the self-preservation instinct, marketing must preserve and protect the well-being of the suprasystem. Thus, it is enlightened self-interest rather than pure altruism that must guide marketing. This enlightened self-interest must give rise to a general strategy of social responsibility. This strategy must have two major features: (1) it must have a total systems approach and hence must deal with the six pathological conditions, elimination of which will help the system's self-optimization; and (2) it must be proactive rather than reactive in its adjustment efforts. Proactivity in this case will prevent probable damage, risk, danger, or other costly alternatives to the enhancement of the prevailing QOL. These two features are interrelated in such a way that the second feature cannot be a reality unless the first feature materializes.

SUMMARY

This chapter takes the position that, as a market economy, we have gotten very far away from Adam Smith's market conditions. The invisible hands that may be in action in the present market are not likely to take the economy and bring it to the conditions that prevailed in Adam Smith's times. The economy, left alone, is likely to get even further away from the conditions described by Adam Smith and classical economists. As the market gets away from perfect conditions to much less than perfect conditions, only the privileged few or some special groups benefit instead of the whole society. This is due to marketing pathology. Pathological conditions in marketing are caused by at least six factors: (1) inadequate inputs, (2) inappropriate inputs, (3) inadequate information, (4) maladaptive marketing philosophy, (5) abnormal production processes, and (6) abnormalities in internal marketing information.

Elimination of marketing pathology is related to social responsibility in marketing. Social responsibility is interpreted as the duty and accountability of marketing. In that sense, marketing will enhance the QOL for the society as a whole. In order to accomplish this goal, it will eliminate the pathological conditions and bring the economy closer to the conditions that prevailed in Adam Smith's times.

REFERENCES

Alderson, Wroe. 1957. *Marketing and Executive Action* Homewood, IL: Richard D. Irwin.

Alderson, Wroe. 1965. *Dynamic Marketing Behavior: A Functionalist Theory of Marketing.* Homewood, IL: Richard D. Irwin.

Engel, James F., Roger D. Blackwell, and Paul K. Miniard. 1990. *Consumer Behavior.* Chicago: Dryden Press.

Hartley, Robert F. 1986. *Marketing Mistakes.* New York: John Wiley and Sons.

Kassarjian, Harold E. 1986. "Consumer Research: Some Recollections and Commentary." In *Advances in Consumer Research* 13, edited by Richard J. Lutz, 6–8. Provo, UT: ACR.

Levitt, Theodore. 1960. "Marketing Myopia." *Harvard Business Review* (July–August):24–47.

Levitt, Theodore. 1975. "The Retrospective Commentary." *Harvard Business Review* (September–October):26–32.

Miller, James G. 1978. *Living Systems*. New York: McGraw-Hill.

Nader, Ralph. 1957. *Unsafe at Any Speed*. New York: Pocket Books.

The New Webster's Dictionary. 1986. New York: Lexicon Publications.

Samli, A. Coskun, and M. Joseph Sirgy. 1982. "Social Responsibility in Marketing: An Analysis and Synthesis." In *Marketing Theory: A Philosophy of Science Perspective*, edited by R. F. Bush and S. D. Hunt, 250–254. Chicago: AMA.

Smith, Adam. 1779. *Wealth of Nations*. London: George Routledge.

2 | Social Responsibility: A Historical Perspective

INTRODUCTION

Social responsibility in marketing has been discussed somewhat extensively in current years. Social scientists, economists, marketing specialists, and social critics on and off have been critical of marketing behavior and encouraged or urged corrective action. Others have tried to help marketing to be more far-reaching and socially responsible.

However, early efforts in trying to bring attention to social responsibility issues are sketchy at best and too few to be of value. Many of them were indirect and perhaps only somewhat related to marketing. This chapter presents a brief discussion of some of these attempts and organizes these attempts in a systematic manner.

THE EARLY EFFORTS

A number of earlier works can be considered closely related to social responsibility. Many of them had certain key issues that are related to social responsibility in marketing. Among these are Veblen's *The Theory of the Leisure Class* (1953), Toynbee's ideas of wasteful consumption (1966), and Galbraith's *The Affluent Society* (1958). In all three works, references have been made to wasteful and perhaps, at times, dangerous consumption patterns.

Galbraith, for instance, alluded to the fact that as a society "we are committed by obsolescent thought to a tense and humorless pursuit of goods and to a fantastic and potentially dangerous effort to manufacture wants as rapidly as we make goods. We are impelled to invest too much in things and not enough in people" (1958, cover jacket). He went on to say that satisfaction from the increasing stock of the individual's goods does not diminish particularly if these goods change and vary. Thus, he indicates that production and consumption could go beyond the boundaries of being reasonable. The wasteful and unnecessary consumption effectively is implied (Galbraith 1958).

The Theory of the Leisure Class by Veblen (1953) deals with the premise that the leisure class is involved in "conspicuous consumption." As the leisure class shows more evidence of conspicuous consumption, the more status it gains. This, again, is related to irresponsible production and consumption that, in time, can cause long-term environmental problems and depletion of valuable natural resources.

Perhaps one of the most important early efforts is attributed to Upton Sinclair, whose book, *The Jungle* (1906), made a significant contribution to the very early consumerism movement in America. Sinclair's book was so significant that it was a best-seller in its time. It was translated into seventeen languages and often was an assigned reading book in American history classes. Upton Sinclair described the conditions in factories, particularly in the meat-processing industry, as dismal. Sinclair considered his book "as part of the process of working-class liberation" (1906, xiii). He called for better quality controls and work conditions.

The early efforts over and beyond those already mentioned can be classified into four categories (Samli and Sirgy 1982): political, legal, popular, and academic.

Political Efforts

Although many cases considered by the Federal Trade Commission (FTC) and the Food and Drug Administration (FDA) have had social responsibility implications, the turning point of social responsibility in the political arena was John F. Kennedy's historic speech before the Congress in 1963 (Kennedy 1963). In that speech, he established the four basic rights for the American consumer: to choose, to be protected, to be informed, and to be heard. These rights are discussed further in Chapter 4. This beginning set the tone of the nationwide consumer protection movement. This movement is made possible by the emergence of the Offices of Consumer Affairs throughout the United States. These offices and others like them explore consumer problems as they occur and as consumers bring problematic issues to these agencies.

Legal Efforts

One of the earliest legal efforts is related to the 1906 pure food and drug act that is claimed to be an outcome of Sinclair's *The Jungle* (1906). Following political efforts, numerous pieces of legislation have emerged dealing primarily with all four of the issues set forth by President Kennedy. Of course, based on these four basic rights, subsequently many new issues emerged and legislative action was taken to cope with these new issues. Among these are:

Truth in lending laws, which made sure that consumers knew how much interest they were paying for borrowed money

Unit pricing, which enabled consumers to compare price advantages of different brands

Disclosure of the contents of canned foodstuffs, which enabled consumers to stay away from certain additives and preservatives

Flammable fabric laws, which enabled consumers to determine the degree of fire danger in various clothing merchandise

In almost all of these cases and many others, the legal action was taken long after many consumer problems occurred and much grief was experienced by many people. Thus, much of the early activity can be termed reactive rather than proactive.

Popular Efforts

Perhaps a most important first private effort can be traced to a nonfiction best-seller in the early 1960s. Vance Packard's *The Waste Makers* (1960) illustrated that particular types of "planned obsolescence" create significant levels of waste that unduly tax our natural resources and contribute only to illusion-generating efforts to improve the quality of life in the society. Packard identified three types of obsolescence: (1) obsolescence of function, (2) obsolescence of quality, and (3) obsolescence of desirability.

The first type of obsolescence—the functional type—could be very constructive for the society if it is planned carefully and if it is an indication of progress rather than just waste. When old-fashioned phonographs became hi-fi, then stereo, and eventually sound systems, there was more progress than waste. However, if the functional changes are designed not necessarily to improve the product but to entice the consumer to buy more goods somewhat unnecessarily, then there may be more waste than progress.

The second type of obsolescence relates to planning a product's breaking down or wearing out. From hand soaps to light bulbs, there have been such developments for many products that are used daily. Packard used a quotation from Gordon Lippincott, one of the nation's leading industrial designers at the time. Lippincott stated in 1958: "Manufacturers have downgraded quality and upgraded complexity. The poor consumer is going crazy" (Packard 1960, 57). As early as 1936, the same ideas prevailed. In fact, a *Printer's Ink* article reflected the situation in the title of an article: "Outmoded Durability: If Merchandise Does Not Wear Out Faster, Factories Will Be Idle, People Unemployed" (Packard 1960, 58). Many other similar discussions in favor of less-durable products ensued.

Finally, obsolescence of desirability relates to a situation in which the product is sound and still performing well. However, the product is not desirable anymore because it is "worn out" in the minds of consumers because of changes in styling. Most fashion products (such as apparel) and those products that are subject to yearly style changes (such as automobiles) deal with this aspect of obsolescence. Packard, by bringing these and many other concepts to the fore and warning the society about the dangers of waste, tried, indirectly, to contribute to the social responsibility aspects of marketing.

About the same time as Packard, Ralph Nader, a dynamic young lawyer, started making the headlines about consumer protection issues. In his book, *Unsafe at Any Speed* (1957), he presented a critical review of automobiles and tires as being unsafe and as causing around 26,000 deaths a year (Nader 1957). This work led to Congressional auto safety hearings that further led to emergence of the Highway Safety Act of 1966.

Environmental concerns and ecological considerations found

their starts with the book, *Silent Spring*, by Rachel Carson (1962). The book dwelled upon the author's extreme concern about the indiscriminate use of chemicals, which were destroying the environment. Rachel Carson's work was substantially more ahead of its time than those mentioned in this section. Her book and her position were ridiculed by the mass media as well as the business sector. Her position was that spring was becoming increasingly silent because of the chemicals, pesticides and insecticides that were killing wildlife.

Finally, Jessica Millford created a lot of publicity with her book, *The American Way of Dying,* which attacked the funeral home industry (1963). She pointed out that some industries have a certain implicit monopoly power in that they take advantage of consumers. In such industries as funeral homes, the situation is particularly bad because the industry puts a substantial amount of pressure, particularly on weak and vulnerable individuals, to buy expensive and unnecessary services, thus indirectly counteracting consumer protection and consumer information efforts.

Academic Efforts

The perceived social responsibility of marketing in the 1950s and early 1960s did not particularly parallel other indirect efforts mentioned thus far. Laden with the traditional view of caveat emptor (let the buyer beware), marketing's general orientation in those days was that marketing fulfills its responsibility by satisfying consumer needs through the availability of products and services that are provided efficiently and profitably (Beckman 1958). This position emphasized a socially inactive position for marketing. It put all the responsibility or the burden on the market system and assumed the existence of a market system that is very close to Adam Smith's market (Smith 1779).

However, the realization of the lack of perfectness in the economic system persuaded some scholars to deal with the social responsibilities of marketing and to treat marketing as a social instrument transmitting the standards of living of the society. As such, they again dealt with marketing's social responsibility issue indirectly. Some scholars emphasized marketing efficiency (Beckman 1958) and others ethical behavior in marketing (Kelley 1963). These early attempts led into a prolific era of exploration of the broader dimensions of marketing that included many aspects of social responsibility (Samli and Sirgy 1982).

EARLY EXPLORATIONS OF SOCIAL RESPONSIBILITY POST-1960s

Different treatments of social responsibility during the late 1960s and 1970s can be explored along at least four different dimensions: indirect implications, normative characteristics, specific social responsibilities, and social responsiveness (Samli and Sirgy 1982). Exhibit 2-1 illustrates these four dimensions.

Indirect Implications

The early 1960s witnessed a heated debate on the broader dimensions of marketing. In an effort to establish proper parameters for

Exhibit 2-1
Social Responsibility in Marketing during the 1960s and 1970s

	Approximate Dates
1. Indirect Implications	(Late 1960s and early 1970s)
Broader Dimensions of Marketing	
More Depth of Marketing	
Social Change in Marketing	
2. Normative Characteristics of Marketing	(Mid 1970s)
Marketing and the Poor	(Early 1960s-Late 1960s)
Consumer Protection	(Early 1960s-Early 1980s)
Consumer Information	(Late 1960s-Mid 1980s)
3. Specific Social Responsibilities	
Marketing and the Poor	(Early 1960s to late 1960s)
Consumer Protection	(Early 1960s to early 1980s)
Consumer Information	(Early 1960s to date)
4. Socially Responsive Marketing	
Resources	(Mid 1970s to early 1980s)
Ecological Implications	(Mid 1960s to date)

marketing, David Luck (1969) and others maintained that marketing is a microprocess and is used primarily for selling and profit making. On the other hand, Kotler and Levy (1969), Kotler (1972), Bagozzi (1974), and others maintained that marketing's parameters are much broader. Because the marketing process is applicable to many nonprofit undertakings, its impact is very far-reaching. For example, the private university tries to attract good students, the hospital enhances its viability in the marketplace by improving its image, the church attempts to maintain and increase its congregation, the opera company makes an effort to offset its losses by increasing its promotional activities. Such organizations as the YMCA, Salvation Army, Girl Scouts, or U.S. Armed Forces all are involved heavily in marketing activities. These nonprofit organizations have been trying to improve their images, amass more support, and gain a greater degree of legitimacy (Kotler 1979). Needless to say, the use of marketing by nonprofit organizations paralleled the growth in marketing awareness and treatment of social responsibility issues.

As Luck and others maintained that marketing is limited, it implied that the market will function to approximate Adam Smith's market without marketing's help. The second group acknowledged that marketing is much more far-reaching than many others claimed. Thus, the second group assumed that the responsibility to approximate the outcome of Adam Smith's market's performance was to be shifted to marketing rather than the market itself. This also implied that marketing must take a proactive posture rather than putting all of its faith in the market and being inactive.

The deepening of the marketing concept has been described by Enis (1973) in terms of developing operational marketing theories and testing them in real marketing situations. He argued that the gap between marketing theory and practice can and should be narrowed. It is implied that all the attempts to broaden the marketing concept also can be redirected in terms of depth. Thus, a stance is presented in regard to developing theories regarding marketing's social responsibilities and applying them so that marketing will have a far-reaching impact (Samli and Sirgy 1982).

Another indirect implication of the idea of social responsibility in marketing is the use of marketing as a social change agent. As Kotler and Zaltman (1971) suggested, the change agent will practice marketing and will have a research unit and a planning unit. These units, through the four P's (i.e., product, price, place, and promotion), bring about social change. Again, social change could come about through the marketing of a social cause, say promoting the United Way or introducing a paper recycling process. Particularly in the case of paper recycling, marketing practices have a certain implied social role and responsibility (Fox and Kotler 1980). Marketing's use as a social change agent once again implies proactive marketing as opposed to inactive marketing. Proactive marketing functions in the direction of making up for the deficiency between the present market and Adam Smith's market, as opposed to putting faith in the present market to reverse itself to Adam Smith's market.

Normative Characteristics of Marketing

Exhibit 2-1 illustrates normative characteristics of marketing as the second dimension of the late 1960s and 1970s era of social responsibility in marketing. This dimension is related to the efforts of those who have attempted to establish the normative characteristics of marketing. Earlier efforts in this area have been in the direction of establishing ethical constraints for marketing. Bartels (1967), for instance, examined the anatomy of marketing decisions that have ethical implications.

A profound effort about the normative implications of marketing was put forth by Shelby Hunt (1971). He discussed the normative aspects of marketing vis-à-vis the nonprofit sector. As normative aspects of marketing are established for the nonprofit sector, strong implications for social responsibility in marketing also have emerged. Robin (1970, 1979) also attempted to establish the constraints of marketing and its normative dimensions.

Fisk (1974a) presented an ambitious attempt in establishing specific norms for marketing process and/or marketing decision implementation on the basis of social priorities. This effort provided a different set of marketing norms. Other attempts have been made by El-Ansary (1979), Lazer (1969), Lavidge (1970), and Arndt (1978), among others, that again established norms and parameters for marketing. By establishing norms and parameters, all these attempts expressed some need for social responsibility in marketing.

Specific Social Responsibilities

During the mid-1960s and through the present day, there have been some specific issues in which marketing has taken certain positions. These issues are related to specific social responsibilities of marketing. Three such issues are identified and discussed briefly here: marketing and the poor, consumer protection, and consumer information (Samli and Sirgy 1982).

Marketing and the poor issues have been considered by a number of marketing scholars (Sturdivant 1968; Goodman 1968; Samli 1969). In these explorations, two closely related issues particularly stood out. First, it was argued that the poor pay more and, hence, marketing practices must be reversed to alleviate this situation or otherwise marketing is favoring only certain groups of people at the expense of others (Caplowitz 1963, Samli 1969). The second issue was related to specific discriminatory practices against the poor (Sturdivant 1968; Samli 1969; Berry 1974). Once again, a marketing position had been taken against such practices that create consumer dissatisfaction at the individual level and inequity at the societal level (Sturdivant 1968; Samli 1971; Andreasen 1976).

Consumer protection activity gained strong impetus after Nader's book, *Unsafe at Any Speed* (1957). The primary roles that have been played by the FTC and FDA are related primarily to consumer protection. The two organizations are given the major tasks of providing a safe atmosphere for the consumer by eliminating unfair or deceptive business policies and practices, and providing safe food as well as drug options. Regarding unfair or deceptive business practices, three areas of activity have been identified: advertising substantiation, corrective advertising, and product information (Wilkie and Gardner 1974). The first area provided substantiation for competitive copy claims. The second area attempted to rectify competitive advantages improperly obtained through deceptive advertising. The third area provided consumers with information to help improve purchasing decisions.

In conjunction with consumer protection, Samli and Sirgy (1982) identified five areas needing more protective legislation. These areas directly or indirectly emerged in the 1970s (Winter 1972). First, there should be more safety regulations. Since the 1980s, there has been some activity in this area, most importantly the automobile safety belt regulations. Second, false advertising must be suppressed. Little progress has taken place in this area. Third, more and better standards of uniformity must be established. Little progress has taken place in this area except perhaps the lemon laws that are used widely in the auto industry to protect the consumer against buying a "lemon" (Bernbach 1962). Fourth, specific information must be disseminated to protect the consumer without jeopardizing a firm's competitive position. Unit pricing for groceries and disclosure of the chemicals and additives in foodstuffs are some of the activities in this area since the 1980s. Fifth, consumers must receive warnings about dangerous products. Since the 1980s, in addition to warnings on cigarettes, a number of similar warnings have been put on drugs and other substances.

Finally, consumer education or information is concerned with developing consumers' capabilities to become better shoppers by dealing with complex purchasing problems effectively (Wilkie and Gardner 1974). After much pressure, truth in lending, truth in labeling, and so on, have come into being as information-providing measures for the consumer. Additional attempts have been made to provide information on prescription drugs by contrasting brands and generic drugs (Burack 1967). Establishing standards in consumer goods (Callazzo 1966) and improving warranty practices (Feldman 1971) also were among these attempts. However, these attempts and many others are hardly adequate for modern American society in which the complexity of the consumer's life has been increasing almost exponentially.

Socially Responsive Marketing

Samli and Sirgy (1982) stated that until the early 1970s marketing encouraged more and, perhaps, sometimes unnecessary utilization of resources, wasting and promoting products that are primarily heavy resource users. It was until that time that marketing encouraged planned obsolescence and such gimmicks as "no deposit, no return" bottles. A number of efforts were put forth exploring the problems of resource depletion and pollution. These efforts tried to reduce the unwanted environmental impacts of marketing decisions by providing other managerial decision alternatives (Henion and Kinnear 1976; Fisk 1974b; Fisk, Arndt and Gronhaug 1978). As ecological issues became of greater concern, some marketing scholars started advocating responsible marketing (Murphy and Enis 1978). Murphy and Enis stated (1978, 260):

Public policy could guide marketers in making such decisions so as to improve long-run social welfare . . . for example, the State of Oregon taxes all beer and soft drink containers to compensate for the resources used by the industry and the resulting pollution. . . . This approach could be broadened . . . by taxing all packages in accordance with their social costs and benefits.

Two of the most significant areas regarding ecology are the automotive and detergent industries (Rukeyser 1972). Both industries have made significant improvements as they exercise socially responsive marketing. However, their social responsiveness has been from without rather than from within. A three-layer hierarchy of pressure has caused socially responsive behavior. Exhibit 2-2 illustrates this process. Because of the concerns of large consumer

Exhibit 2-2
Pressures for Social Responsiveness

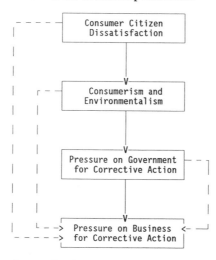

Source: Samli and Sirgy 1982, p. 253.

groups, many customers have started feeling uneasy about buying cars or detergents that are unsound ecologically. Both consumer groups and prospective customer groups have pressured businesses and the government directly to do something about the situation. The outcome has been such that government directly and indirectly put pressure on certain industries. Direct pressure was brought about by lawsuits by such government agencies as the FDA and the FTC. Indirect pressures were created by moral suasion exercised by government officials, marketing scholars, and consumer advocates (Samli and Sirgy 1982).

Thus, marketing, under social pressures, has become more socially responsive. This social responsiveness has been in the areas of scarce resources and other consumer and ecological issues, including air and water pollution, consumer education, and consumer protection.

As can be seen from the discussion thus far, during the late 1960s and 1970s there was some ferment in regard to the social responsibilities of marketing (Perry 1976). However, two major problems plagued these activities. First, activities and thoughts relating to the social responsibility of marketing have been very fragmented. There was no systematic or planned activity in the marketing discipline to treat the problem in a holistic manner (i.e., consider the well-being of the total society and look at the marketing discipline as a whole and establishing major relationships between the two). Second, marketing practice, at best, has been socially responsive, not necessarily socially responsible. It has reacted to pressures instead of being proactive and exercising a socially responsible posture rather than simply responding to pressure.

Because of these two factors, fragmented and responsive behavior, many gaps in social responsibility remained untouched. In fact, as our society became more complex, many unresolved social responsibility areas emerged. New cancer-causing substances, such new environmental effects as the greenhouse effect, and new consumer protection and consumer legislation issues have surfaced during the past decade and a half.

Just why is it that marketing's social responsibility activities have been so sketchy? The answer, at least partially, lies in the development, perception, and implementation of the marketing concept.

THE EVOLUTION OF THE MARKETING CONCEPT

The marketing concept surfaced in the mid-1950s. In essence, it articulated a management philosophy of customer satisfaction. It advocates that the management must put all of its resources together to satisfy the customers in the target markets and be rewarded in terms of profits based on the degree of satisfying the customer's needs. King defined the marketing concept as "a managerial philosophy concerned with the mobilization, utilization and control of total corporate effort for the purpose of helping consumers solve selected problems in ways compatible with planned enhancement of the profit position of the firm" (1965, 85).

Although the marketing concept is powerful and very workable, the way it was perceived and implemented by the top management left something to be desired. Numerous authors maintained that the marketing concept encourages short-run orientation and hence has stifled the long-run development and competitive advantage of U.S. industry (Wind and Robertson 1983, Hayes and Abernathy 1980, Bennett and Cooper 1981). They claimed that because of the marketing concept American businesses are so preoccupied with short-term market opportunities that they will not make higher-risk long-term investments in new technologies. Furthermore, they maintained that the marketing concept caused management to de-emphasize true innovations and products in favor of other elements of marketing mix, elements that can be manipulated very successfully in the short run, but that will leave the business vulnerable in the long run.

All of these objections to the marketing concept stem from how the management conceptualized and implemented the concept. When Kotler said: "In short, the marketing concept says find wants and fill them, rather than create products and sell them" (1988, 17), he did not mean find wants and fill them now. However, the concept was misconstrued and was misused. American management's preoccupation with the short run and quick profits caused questionable marketing practices and consumer discontent. Finally, one additional flaw in the implementation of the marketing concept has contributed further to consumer discontent. This is related to the marketing concept's orientation to satisfy the needs of the target customers. As this concept becomes implemented, the rest of the society, in essence citizen consumers other than the customers of the firm, are not taken into consideration. Thus, while the firm tries to satisfy its customers' needs, it virtually ignores the rest of the society. Thus, cigarette manufacturers ignored nonsmokers and producers of environmentally unsafe products did not do much about their products.

This overall series of criticisms about marketing orientation of firms in the society is an indication of less-than-adequate performance of the marketing concept. This inadequacy has facilitated the advancement of consumerism in American society.

THE CONSUMERISM MOVEMENT

Aaker and Day identified consumerism as the "contemporary movement, launched in the mid-1960s by the concern triggered indirectly by Rachel Carson and directly by Ralph Nader's auto safety investigation and by President Kennedy's efforts to establish the four rights of consumers: the right to safety, to be informed, to choose and to be heard" (1982, 2).

They further stated that "consumerism encompasses the evolving activities of government, business, independent organizations and concerned consumers to protect and enhance the right of consumers" (1982, 2).

The customer-versus-the-consumer dichotomy has led to the development of the consumerism movement in American society. This dichotomy started with certain marketing practices geared to the satisfaction of customers at the expense of other consumers. Passive smoking is one such case. Smokers' and nonsmokers' interests clearly are in opposition. The dichotomy generated at least nine specific problem situations: (1) disillusionment with the system, (2) the performance gap, (3) the consumer information gap, (4) antagonism toward advertising, (5) impersonal and unresponsive marketing institutions, (6) invasions of privacy, (7) declining living standards, (8) special problems of the disadvantaged, and (9) different views of the marketplace (Aaker and Day 1982). These are discussed briefly below.

1. *Disillusionment with the System.* Aaker and Day (1982) proposed that an imbalance of power among components of our soci-

ety may have encouraged this trend. They further hypothesized that marketers were among those whose power was resented. They maintained that the large number of measures taken to strengthen the consumer's rights is a support for this hypothesis because these measures attempted to improve the consumer's bargaining position.

2. *The Performance Gap.* What consumers expect from a product and its performance may not be quite what the product may deliver. Consumers' expectations have been rising steadily because of competition and competitive advertising. However, improvements also make products more complex, and complexity may cause minor but irritating malfunctions. This may lead to increasing dissatisfaction on the part of consumers.

3. *The Consumer Information Gap.* Not only has the number of products from which the consumer must choose grown enormously, but their complexity also has increased substantially. A supermarket has over 10,000 different items. A department store may have 40,000–50,000 different products. Furthermore, these products are now more complex. Their evaluation by the consumer may take different forms. They could be evaluated by consumers along the lines of performance or health and environmental impact, among others. In addition to more and complex production, the lack of knowledgeable sales people in large retail establishments, coupled with reduced shopping time on the part of consumers, makes it impossible to narrow the information gap, let alone eliminate it.

4. *Antagonism toward Advertising.* Advertising expenditures are increasing constantly. Even though it is a crucial part of the overall consumer information system, consumers are somewhat skeptical of the information obtained through advertising. They are not sure about the truthfulness as well as the usefulness of advertising.

5. *Impersonal and Unresponsive Marketing Institutions.* With the increase of self-service retailing, declining knowledgeability of sales representatives, expanding demand for complex services, along with extensive use of computers, it has become increasingly difficult for the consumer to follow a recourse for satisfaction. Much of the time, consumers are far removed from the company management and do not know how to complain or have adjustments made to their purchases.

6. *Invasions of Privacy.* With the expansion of telecommunications and computer technologies, there has been an increasing pos-

sibility of intrusion on individual privacy. Increased capacity for storing and retrieving information makes it possible for information to be used against the consumer in an abusive manner. The information may be used for wrong purposes, unfairly, or even incorrectly.

7. *Declining Living Standards.* The overall performance of the American market system has not been very steady. It has caused a growing gap between the rich and the poor. Furthermore, it created a large number of homeless and poor people who are not in the mainstream market. The overall attitude of consumers has been one of pessimism.

8. *Special Problems of the Disadvantaged.* During the past two decades or so, the disadvantaged in our society have become worse off than before. Among the disadvantaged are the young, the old, and the poor. Research indicated that the disadvantaged got progressively worse off than the rest of the society.

9. *Different Views of the Marketplace.* In essence, marketplace and marketing are interpreted differently by different groups. Critics of marketing took the position that marketing's role basically is to persuade or seduce the less-than-willing consumers to buy. They claimed that marketing has gotten too much power. On the other hand, the promarketing position has been that marketing has the ability to identify and serve consumer needs.

All nine problem situations generated some degree of antimarketing sentiment. They therefore facilitated the development and strengthening of the consumer movement that still continues.

SUMMARY

This chapter explores some of the early works relating to social responsibility in marketing. These early works, at best, have been sketchy. However, they provided a direction to this very important area of exploration.

The first part of early efforts are discussed in terms of political, legal, popular, and academic efforts. The later phases of early efforts also are discussed in four categories: (1) indirect implications, (2) normative characteristics of marketing, (3) specific social responsibilities, and (4) socially responsive marketing.

The emergence and acceptance of the marketing concept also

contributed to the social responsibility area. The concept, it is maintained, was not well understood and not implemented correctly.

Finally, the consumerism movement started because of the partial failure of the marketing concept. It basically tried to rectify the lacking social responsibility component in the marketing practices.

REFERENCES

Aaker, David A., and George Day. 1982. "A Guide to Consumerism." In *Consumerism*, edited by David A. Aaker and George Day, 2–20. New York: The Free Press.

Andreasen, Alan. 1976. "The Differing Nature of Consumerism in the Ghetto." *Journal of Consumer Affairs* (Winter):179–190.

Arndt, J. 1978. "How Broad Should the Marketing Concept Be?" *Journal of Marketing* (January):101–103.

Bagozzi, Richard. 1974. "Marketing As an Organized Behavioral System of Exchange," *Journal of Marketing* 38:77–78.

Bartels, Robert. 1967. "A Model for Ethics in Marketing." *Journal of Marketing* 31 (January):20–25.

Beckman, Theodore N. 1958. "The Value Added Concept as Applied to Marketing and Its Implications." In *Marketing in Transition*, edited by Alfred L. Seelye. New York: Harper & Brothers.

Bennett, R. C., and R. G. Cooper. 1981. "The Misuse of Marketing: An American Tragedy." *Business Horizons* (November–December):51–61.

Bernbach, V. S. 1962. "Is Advertising Morally Responsible?" *Yale Daily News* (Special Issue).

Berry, Leonard. 1974. "The Low Income Marketing System: An Overview." In *Consumerism: Search for the Consumer Interest*, edited by David A. Aaker and George S. Day. New York: Free Press.

Burack, Richard. 1967. *The Handbook of Prescription Drugs*. New York: Pantheon Books.

Callazzo, Charles J., Jr. 1966. "Effects of Income Upon Shopping Attitudes and Frustrations." *Journal of Retailing* (Spring).

Caplowitz, David. 1963. *The Poor Pay More*. New York: Free Press.

Carson, Rachel. 1962. *Silent Spring*. Boston: Houghton Mifflin.

El-Ansary, Adel. 1979. "The General Theory of Marketing Revisited." In *Conceptual and Theoretical Developments in Marketing*, edited by I. C. Farrell, L. Brown, and C. Lamb, 399–407. Chicago: American Marketing Association.

Enis, Ben. 1973. "Deepening the Concept of Marketing." *Journal of Marketing* 37 (October):57–62.

Feldman, Lawrence P. 1971. "Societal Adaptation. A New Challenge for Marketing." *Journal of Marketing* 35 (July):35–44.

Fisk, George, ed. 1974a. *Marketing and Social Priorities*. Chicago: American Marketing Association.

Fisk, George. 1974b. *Marketing and Ecological Crisis*. New York: Harper and Row.

Fisk, George, Johan Arndt, and Kyell Gronhaug. 1978. *Future Directions of Marketing*. Cambridge, MA: Marketing Science Institute, Report 78-104.

Fox, K. A., and P. Kotler. 1980. "The Marketing of Social Causes: The First 10 Years." *Journal of Marketing* 44:24–33.

Galbraith, John Kenneth. 1958. *The Affluent Society*. Boston: Houghton Mifflin.

Goodman, Charles. 1968. "Do the Poor Pay More?" *Journal of Marketing* (January):18–24.

Hayes, R. H., and W. J. Abernathy. 1980. "Managing Our Way to Economic Decline." *Harvard Business Review* (July–August):67–77.

Henion, Karl E., and Thomas Kinnear (eds.). 1976. *Ecological Marketing*. Chicago: American Marketing Association.

Hunt, Shelby. 1971. "The Morphology of Theory of the General Theory of Marketing." *Journal of Marketing* 35 (April).

Kelley, Eugene. 1963. "Ethical Behavior in Marketing." In *Toward Scientific Marketing*, edited by Stephen A. Greyser. Chicago: American Marketing Association.

Kennedy, John F. 1963. "Consumer Advisory Council: First Report." Executive Office of the President, Washington, DC: U.S. Government Printing Office, October.

King, Robert L. 1965. "The Marketing Concept." In *Science in Marketing*, edited by George Schwartz, 70–97. New York: Wiley.

Kotler, Philip. 1972. "A Generic Concept of Marketing." *Journal of Marketing* (April):7–15.

Kotler, Philip. 1979. "Strategies for Introducing Marketing into Non-Profit Organizations." *Journal of Marketing* 43 (January):37–44.

Kotler, Philip. 1988. *Marketing Management*. Englewood Cliffs, NJ: Prentice-Hall.

Kotler, Philip, and Sidney J. Levy. 1969. "Broadening the Concept of Marketing." *Journal of Marketing* 33 (January):55–56.

Kotler, Philip, and Gerald Zaltman. 1971. "Social Marketing: An Approach to Planned Social Change." *Journal of Marketing* 37 (July): 3–12.

Lazer, William. 1969. "Marketing's Changing Social Relationships." *Journal of Marketing* 33 (January):3–9.

Lavidge, Robert J. 1970. "The Growing Responsibilities of Marketing." *Journal of Marketing* 34 (January):17–23.

Luck, David J. 1969. "Broadening the Concept of Marketing — Too Far." *Journal of Marketing* 33 (July):53–55.

Millford, Jessica. 1963. *The American Way of Dying*. New York: Simon and Schuster.

Moyer, Reed. 1972. *Macromarketing, A Social Perspective*. New York: John Wiley & Sons.

Murphy, Patrick E., and Ben M. Enis. 1978. "Let's Hear the Case Against Brand X." In *Consumerism: Search for the Consumer Interest*, 3d ed., edited by David A. Aaker and George S. Day, 259–267. New York: Free Press.

Nader, Ralph. 1957. *Unsafe at Any Speed*. New York: Pocket Books.

Packard, Vance. 1960. *The Waste Makers*. New York: David McKay.

Perry, Donald. 1976. *Social Marketing Strategies*. Pacific Palisades, CA: Goodyear Publishing Co.

Robin, Donald P. 1970. "Toward a Normative Science in Marketing." *Journal of Marketing* (October):63–66.

Robin, Donald P. 1979. "A Useful Scope for Marketing." *Journal of Academy of Marketing Science* (Summer):228–238.

Rukeyser, William S. 1972. "Facts and Foam in the Row Over Phosphates." *Fortune* (February):55–72.

Samli, A. Coskun. 1969. "Differential Price for the Rich and Poor." *University of Washington Business Review* (Summer):111–113.

Samli, A. Coskun. 1971. "DeFacto Price Discrimination in the Food Purchases of the Rural Poor." *Journal of Retailing* (Fall):65–73.

Samli, A. Coskun, and M. Joseph Sirgy. 1982. "Social Responsibility in Marketing." In *Marketing Theory: A Philosophy of Science Perspective*, edited by R. F. Bush and S. D. Hunt, 250–254. Chicago: American Marketing Association.

Sinclair, Upton. 1906. *The Jungle*. New York: The New American Library of World Literature.

Smith, Adam. 1779. *Wealth of Nations*. London: George Routledge.

Sturdivant, Frederick D. 1968. "Better Deal for Ghetto Shoppers." *Harvard Business Review* 46 (March–April):130–139.

Toynbee, Arnold. 1966. *America and the World Revolution*. New York: Oxford University Press.

Veblen, Thorstein. 1953. *The Theory of the Leisure Class*. New York: Mentor Books.

Wilkie, William L., and David M. Gardner. 1974. "The Role of Marketing

Research in Public Policy Decision Making." *Journal of Marketing* 38 (January):38–47.

Wind, Y. J., and T. S. Robertson. 1983. "Marketing Strategy: New Directions for Theory and Research." *Journal of Marketing* (Spring):12–25.

Winter, Ralph K. 1972. "The Consumer Advocate versus the Consumer." Washington, DC: American Enterprise Institute for Public Policy Research.

3 | Redirection in Social Responsibility

INTRODUCTION

It is mentioned in Chapter 1 that the market system, in its current form, is extremely different from what Adam Smith visualized (Smith 1779). Thus, in order to yield the expected results as foreseen by Adam Smith, the prevailing American market needs additional functions to rectify the situation. Since the expected outcome of Adam Smith's market is not likely to materialize, supplementary activities are necessary to yield the same results. This is the role of marketing. Marketing can make up for the deficiency of the prevailing market and make it perform as if it were Adam Smith's time. From this perspective, marketing can have four distinct roles in the market: (1) negative, (2) inactive, (3) reactive, and (4) proactive. This chapter explores these four separate roles and presents an argument for proactivity.

NEGATIVE MARKETING

In its attempts to generate exchange and distribution, it is not automatic that marketing performs a socially responsible function. In fact, in the absence of the conditions that existed in Adam Smith's era, marketing could be performing in a socially negative way. This performance is discussed in Chapter 2 as marketing pathology. Exhibit 3-1 presents a summary of these pathological con-

Exhibit 3-1
Negative Marketing Caused by Marketing Pathology

Pathological Condition	Marketing Practice Examples
1. Inadequate resource inputs	Product quality deterioration depicted by short-lived lightbulbs, soaps and many other consumer products.
2. Inappropriate forms of inputs	Use of carcinogens and other dangerous substances which may be low cost and enhance the profit picture of the marketer.
3. Inadequate marketing information inputs	Practices leading to marketing unneeded goods, low quality goods, potentially harmful products to the individual and the society as a whole.
4. Maladaptive marketing strategy	Defective or deficient corporate philosophy disabling the organization to respond to external and higher needs prevailing in the market, such as developing environmentally or ecologically dangerous products.
5. Abnormalities in internal product related processes	Developing inferior products by not reading the market needs and by not improving product related processes.
6. Abnormalities in internal market information process	Developing products which are not competitive enough because of not using marketing information properly.

ditions (Samli and Sirgy 1982). Any condition or a combination of these pathological conditions, could cause problems unnecessarily for society as a whole or problems for specific groups of consumers. Similarly, some of the pathological conditions could generate unnecessary profits and an undeserved competitive edge for a firm. This is due to the fact that the market does not function in a perfectly competitive manner. Finally, almost all of the pathological conditions are likely to create excessive social costs that invariably are to be paid by consumers sometime in the future. Thus, negative marketing could take place if the pathological conditions exist and if there is no attempt to correct them. It is difficult to foresee just how harmful this proposed negative marketing could become if it is not stopped; however, it is quite justifiable to assume that it would take us even further from where the prevailing market stands vis-à-vis Adam Smith's market. In other words, almost all basic features of Adam Smith's market in terms of its self-adjusting and optimizing capabilities are likely to disappear. Unchecked or unregulated negative marketing could be self-destructive to the point of total social irresponsibility, along with total danger not only to the economic well-being of the society, but to its environmental and physical well-being.

INACTIVE MARKETING

As opposed to being negative and ruthless, marketing can be strictly inactive. *Inactivity* means not being involved in issues related to social responsibility. In this case, marketing is not involved in negative or positive activities with significant social implications. It is rather difficult to imagine situations in which marketing's social involvement is negligible. However, if marketing is not creating the pathological situations deliberately and if it is not attempting to remedy those pathological situations that already may exist, then clearly marketing is inactive.

Inactive marketing implies marketing's neutrality within the society. Once again, in Adam Smith's market such a neutrality might have been possible; in fact, it might have been sufficient. For the system to function optimally, however, under today's prevailing market conditions, inactive marketing may not be neutral. Inactivity, in this case, is doing nothing about numerous social areas (see Chapters 1 and 2). Such inactivity has been practiced by a myriad of marketing practitioners up to the 1970s. Perhaps it is practiced even today. There are many practitioners who are so concerned (or preoccupied) with the day-to-day conduct of their businesses that they would not take part in socially related projects or be part of ongoing debates about social responsibility. Because of their preoccupation with day-to-day activities, they even may not have developed any level or semblance of social consciousness. In addition, many small practitioners may not have a chance to make an impact on some aspect of social responsibility. The health food stores, for instance, may be selling a product that is not tested adequately or may have certain questionable side effects and the stores may not know it. Similarly, as the choices become more plentiful and consumers buy with less education or information, the chances of making poor purchase decisions increase (Friedman and Rees 1988; Keller and Staelin 1987). Again, moving away from Adam Smith's market conditions continues. This is due to inactive marketing, which again functions de facto as negative marketing.

Inactivity, as described here, in a sense implies a passive negative marketing. This passive negative marketing function is due to the basic premise that with every passing day the present-day market is getting further and further away from Adam Smith's market. Again, assuming this moving away is basically negative, passive marketing is not helping to counteract this movement. Hence, inactive marketing is in essence negative, however, this negativity is indirect.

REACTIVE MARKETING

There are many examples of reactive marketing. For instance, after many years of criticism from environmentalists, McDonald's Corporation decided not to use Styrofoam packaging for its products. The company also started revising its menu and providing healthier products and products containing less fat for its customers. Much of this behavior was in response to changing times and external pressures. When Red Dye No. 2 was identified as a cancer-causing substance, food-processing companies, confectioners, and other companies that used this product abandoned it. Rely tampons became a focal point of attack as a cause of toxic shock syndrome. The producer took the product out of the market. After many years of criticism coming from the general public, some alcoholic beverage manufacturers decided to start advertising campaigns to discourage drinking and driving. After numerous lawsuits because of user deaths, Dalkon Shield intrauterine devices (IUDs) (A. H. Robbins Company) were discontinued. However, the whole episode caused a bankruptcy for the manufacturer.

There are many similar examples illustrating such patterns of reactive marketing. The critical point about reactive marketing is the time that lapses between the beginning of the marketing practice and the subsequent pressures created by certain consumer groups, public opinion, or government agencies. When, for instance, Rely tampons were introduced, it took many months before they were connected to toxic shock syndrome. It was more than 20 years before Dalkon Shield IUDs were banned. From the point of its introduction until the company discontinues it, some public agency bans it, or consumer groups boycott it, a product can cause much damage for the users personally as well as for the society. By the time the manufacturers took Rely tampons out of the market, many people had died. The company had to set aside a very large sum for legal defense, and the whole process disrupted many families' lives. Dalkon Shield IUDs created thousands of cancer victims, many of whom lost their lives.

In all similar cases, the marketing practice follows the pressures caused by the market, by some social institution, or by the law. The reaction of the marketer rectifies the problem but cannot possibly take away or make up for the damage it caused.

Exhibit 3-2 illustrates the reactive marketing process. When the product or service is introduced, there may or may not be enough immediate public reaction. In some cases, medical and scientific evidence against the product or the service accumulates only over time. Of course, this is due partially to less-than-sufficient preliminary research before the product or service is introduced. As the

Exhibit 3-2
Reactive Marketing Process

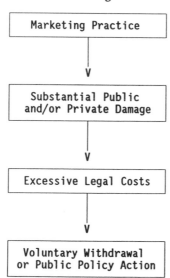

Marketing Practice

V

Substantial Public
and/or Private Damage

V

Excessive Legal Costs

V

Voluntary Withdrawal
or Public Policy Action

evidence builds up and it becomes clear that this product or service is not fit to be used, it may be too late for many people. A public outcry may take place before any serious remedial action occurs. In some cases, in conjunction with the public outcry, excessive legal costs will occur. These costs actually may force the firm into receivership. Thus, the firm not only causes substantial public damage or nuisance for the society, but it actually hurts itself. If, despite the public outcry, the company does not withdraw the product, then, through public policy action, the product could be banned or consumers could be warned.

As can be seen, reactive marketing comes about primarily because of outside pressures that can be legal or political in form. In either case, there may be substantial damage to the society as well as the firm.

PROACTIVE MARKETING

Our discussion, thus far, indicates that the first three marketing forms (i.e., negative, inactive, and reactive marketing) hardly are adequate for societal needs. It is difficult to imagine how the modern American market could function to perform with the same type of adequacy as Adam Smith's market if marketing is taking one of these three social orientations. By the method of elimination, it becomes obvious that marketing must be proactive if the performance of the modern American market is to have a chance to come closer to the performance of Adam Smith's market.

Proactive marketing is illustrated in Exhibit 3-3. The key point in the exhibit, preintroduction product research for social responsibility, is also the key point of proactive marketing. As seen in the exhibit, the evaluation of the social responsibility aspects of a product must begin as the product is conceptualized and developed. At this stage in the game, the evaluation process is internal to the firm with perhaps a minimal amount of external input. A product development group or a creative committee may consider the proposed product's features in terms of its being a potentially socially responsible product. More is said about such a methodology in Chapter 8.

Beyond the conceptual stage, as the product is being developed and its design is adjusted further, an actual test of that product's performance becomes a necessity. As illustrated in Exhibit 3-3, the

are very critical in generating social and private costs, as well as social and private benefits.

SOCIAL COSTS, PRIVATE COSTS, AND MARKETING DECISIONS

Unfortunately, emphasizing the bottom line, by definition, almost is ignoring social costs. Emphasizing the bottom line means being particularly cost conscious. Such cost consciousness will try to minimize all the tangible private costs, and will try to exclude other indirect and extraneous costs. However, if marketing decisions are such that they are causing excessive social costs, society as a whole is losing. Consumers in such cases are not enjoying the quality of life they could enjoy otherwise. It is necessary to realize that any time a marketing decision is made there is a social cost. Unless this cost is minimized, the society cannot optimize its economic activity and consumers cannot enjoy the highest quality of life. Minimization of the social cost is related closely to proactive marketing decisions. Proactivity, by definition, eliminates social costs and optimizes quality of life. It can be concluded that redirection in social responsibility by marketing takes place primarily by switching from inactive or reactive marketing orientation to proactive marketing orientation.

SUMMARY

This chapter makes a distinction among negative, inactive, reactive, and proactive marketing. It is posited that negative marketing is related to marketing pathology. It causes excessive pathological situations within the society. Inactive marketing, de facto, may cause pathological situations and again cause excessive profit losses as well as social and societal problems.

Reactive marketing has a reasonable performance record if compared to the first two alternatives. However, the reaction time may be too long and, therefore, the social costs caused by certain marketing practices may be excessive. Therefore, it is logical that proactive marketing is the way to eliminate poor products and services before they reach the market. Marketing's social responsibility must be directed toward proactivity. The more proactive marketing decisions are, the better off the individual business is, as well as the society as a whole.

REFERENCES

Churchill, Gilbert A. Jr. 1987. *Marketing Research*. Chicago: Dryden Press.

Friedman, Monroe, and Jennifer Rees. 1988. "A Behavioral Science Assessment of Selected Principles of Consumer Education." *Journal of Consumer Affairs* (Winter):284–302.

Keller, Kevin Lane, and Richard Staelin. 1987 "Effects of Quality and Quantity of Information on Decision Effectiveness." *Journal of Consumer Research* (September):200–213.

Parasuraman, A. 1991. *Marketing Research*. Reading, MA: Addison-Wesley.

Samli, A. Coskun, Christian Palda, and Tansu Barker. 1987. "Toward a Mature Marketing Concept." *Sloan Management Review* (Winter):45–51.

Samli, A. Coskun, and M. Joseph Sirgy. 1982. "Social Responsibility in Marketing." In *Marketing Theory: A Philosophy of Science Perspective*, edited by R. F. Bush and S. D. Hunt, 250–254. Chicago: American Marketing Association.

Smith, Adam. 1779. *Wealth of Nations*. London: George Routledge.

4 | The Myth of the Equal Opportunity Consumer

A. Coskun Samli and William C. Wilkinson

INTRODUCTION

Consumers are not equal; what is more, they never will be equal. However, it is desirable to think that one day all consumers will have equal opportunity. At the present time, equal opportunity is strictly a myth. It is obvious that as the society becomes more complex, vulnerable consumer groups are affected more. Some consumers, to begin with, do not have equal opportunity to optimize their purchase decisions and purchase behaviors. There are hardly any direct or indirect forces or agencies to enhance the equal opportunity component of American markets. If uninterrupted, existing trends and conditions are such that the myth will continue and conditions, particularly for certain groups, will get worse. The myth of the equal opportunity consumer is illustrated in Exhibit 4-1. As can be seen from the diagram, increasing monopolies, increasing societal complexity, inadequate information, misuse of resources, excessive short-run orientation, and decreasing competition have a negative impact on American consumers. However, four special groups are particularly influenced adversely: minorities, the less educated, the elderly, and the frail.

Even though in America there are more claims about having freedom and being free than in any other country in the world, the claims fall far short when consumers are considered. This is not saying that America represents a system of slavery or a despotic

Exhibit 4-1
The Myth of the Equal Opportunity Consumer

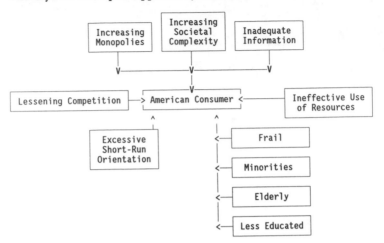

structure; rather, it represents a large mass of typically unequal opportunity consumers. In this chapter, we explore just what it would take to provide equal opportunity to all American consumers rather than a privileged few.

CONSUMERS' WELL-BEING: THE PAST

When John F. Kennedy introduced what subsequently was known as the consumer manifesto, he single-handedly reversed caveat emptor (let the buyer beware), the general practice in the American market system. Up to that point, it was left to the consumer to protect himself or herself. Kennedy proposed four major rights for the consumer: (1) the right to know, (2) the right to choose, (3) the right to be protected, and (4) the right to be heard (Kennedy 1963). These four rights primarily set the tone of modern American consumerism.

During the past several presidential campaigns, the question has been raised, "Are we better off than four years ago?" The answer in a general sense is more negative than affirmative. Just what happened to the American quality of life (QOL) since 1963? Although there is not one single criterion nor is there a perfect measure, many believe that it is not getting any better. In fact, according to many, it is deteriorating. Why should marketing people worry about this? Because if the quality of life is not improving, first, there will be fewer profits to be made by marketers and, second, if the quality of life is not improving, marketing basically is performing less than adequately.

Although Chapter 1 deals with this issue in general terms, it is necessary to explore the forces that may be causing the deterioration of the QOL in America. There are at least five such forces that need to be explored here: (1) our resources are not used quite effectively, (2) complexity of the society is increasing exponentially, (3) information is difficult to get or is less than adequate, (4) emphasis on the short run is becoming more prevalent, and (5) competition in the classical sense is on the decline.

MISALLOCATED (OR MISUSED) RESOURCES

Two underlying factors primarily are causing misallocation of our resources. First, the income distribution is becoming worse, that is, the society is creating a few very rich and many poor at the expense of the middle class. Thus, resources are allocated to cater to the needs of the extreme rich and many poor, resulting in an uneven distribution of resources. For instance, while there is an inadequate supply of low-income housing, there are innumerable expensive luxury housing complexes.

Second, inadequacy of the marketing system to detect and cater to consumer needs systematically and accurately also causes misallocation of resources. While, for instance, a substantial degree of hunger is prevalent in the United States, some farmers still are being paid not to produce. This point is discussed also in Chapter 2 in the exploration of marketing pathologies.

INCREASING SOCIETAL COMPLEXITY

The increasing complexity in our society is related to information explosion. Information generation and dissemination have reached new heights (Naisbitt 1982). The result of this high-tech revolution is very significant for consumer choices as well as the increasing complexity of products, making it more difficult to make good purchase decisions. For instance, as personal computers (PCs) become more powerful and more versatile and as their variety increases, the typical consumer, who is not a computer expert, will be at a disadvantage in making the best choice. By the same token, the consumer who is a computer specialist will develop an undue advantage over average consumers. Thus, as the complexity in the marketplace increases, those who are ahead of such developments or those who can cope with these developments are likely to develop substantial powers, whereas those who are not equally versatile are likely to get even further behind.

Another aspect of the increasing complexity of society reflects itself in some new types of risks that are emerging. Many of these risks did not exist one or two decades ago. Among these risks are environmental, health, safety, and longevity risks.

Environmental risks, among other things, are related to the greenhouse effect, the thinning of the ozone layer, and contamination of water, air, and soil. Almost none of these was a key problem two or three decades ago. As the industrial and technological capabilities of the business sector increase, more sophisticated products find their way to the market. Much of the time, along with sophistication, there is also an increasing environmental offensiveness. From aerosol cans to plastics, a wide variety of products are environmentally offensive, indicating an increasing social cost for everyone when these products are used often and indiscriminantly.

Health risks are related to new diseases and somewhat deteriorating health conditions due to the pressures of modern life. Among the new diseases are acquired immunodeficiency syndrome (AIDS), different varieties of influenzas, newly resurging tuberculosis, and many ailments that may be attributable to smoking, poor diet, and lack of exercise, which are caused by the pressures of modern living.

Safety risks in modern times primarily are related to auto accidents. Some 27,000 auto accidents a year cause many disabling and life-threatening situations. Other types of safety risks are related to increasing violent crime and failure on the part of the society to enforce the laws.

Longevity creates its own risks. Among these is Alzheimer's disease. Older people also become dependent on others, sometimes unscrupulous others. In our society during the past decade or so, there have been more legal questions or investigations about retirement homes and other services for the elderly than ever before. Many other problems are related directly to aging. Most of these problems stem from the fact that the number of the elderly in our society is increasing very fast and the laws, conditions, or even prevailing values are not geared for this fact. Such specific needs of the elderly as recreation, medical care, or housing, necessitate the emergence of many new and different services. Many of these services do not emerge until the needs become a borderline problem. In many other services, until the whole activity is coordinated, there may be many abuses negatively affecting the QOL of the elderly. The appendix at the end of this chapter deals with the QOL of the elderly in greater detail.

Impact on Specific Groups

As the society becomes more complex, the impact on different groups is not quite even. Different groups feel the impact differently and hence there is a different impact on their respective QOLs. Four specific groups are considered briefly here: (1) minorities, (2) the less educated, (3) the elderly, and (4) the frail.

Minorities

Minorities typically are economically disadvantaged. Hispanic Americans and African Americans typically have less-than-average income; they are the last to be hired and first to be fired. Hispanic Americans also have a language handicap that makes them less mobile and impaired as consumers since they have to limit the outlets they can frequent and they cannot establish two-way communication with non-Spanish-speaking merchants. They typically end up paying more for inferior products. Although there are no specific studies testing this hypothesis, it is reasonable to hypothesize that as the society becomes more complex, already disadvantaged minorities have greater difficulty coping and maintaining their status quo. A number of studies allude to the fact that, in addition to their lack of equal opportunity, these groups are discriminated against (Strutton and Tudor 1991; Spratlin 1991). If they already have difficulty making a good choice in purchasing a TV set, it is most likely that they will have greater difficulty in selecting a PC.

The Less Educated

Although minorities and less-educated groups overlap substantially, there are nonminorities who also are less educated. It has been estimated that about 25% of the American population is functionally illiterate. These people are not likely to advance professionally. As the society becomes more complex, they will have greater difficulty even to maintain their relative positions, which already are questionable. As the society becomes more complex, better jobs require more and better training; thus, the less educated do not have a chance to advance.

The Elderly

As the society advances, there are more elderly. This is due to the expanding life span attributable to advanced science. However, it is also true that the birth rate declines as the society becomes more advanced. The increasing number of the elderly is not paralleled by marketing progress. Many needs of the elderly are not taken into account. This is due to the fact that, although their number is increasing, the elderly still do not present a large enough market for some of the products they need. Thus, many marketers may not find this segment profitable enough to cater to some of its specific needs (see the Appendix).

Increasing complexity of the society also has a direct impact on the elderly. First, the elderly have difficulty in developing and retaining their routines, which are essential for their QOL. Second, elderly people have difficulty understanding complex life-styles and commensurate complexities of modern gadgetry. Third, increasing complexity of life has a direct negative impact on the elderly since their ability to cope does not increase.

The Frail

Not enough work is done concerning the frail. There are those who have slightly less-than-average decision-making and problem-solving capabilities. These people are called *frail* in this chapter. This concept is discussed in greater depth in Chapter 5. Research is less than adequate about what happens to these people when the society becomes more complex and decisions become more difficult. It is quite doubtful that they will be able to make good consumer decisions to optimize their QOL. All things being the same, their already quite fragile QOL is likely to deteriorate.

In addition to lacking good decision-making skills, the frail may have distorted risk perception. They may have difficulty understanding the risk involved in a risky product or, similarly, they may exaggerate the risk involved in using a product. In either case, this distorted risk perception further distorts the already weak decision-making capabilities of the frail consumer.

As seen from the brief analysis of these four groups, as the society becomes more complex, their relative QOL are likely to deteriorate because of worsening market conditions and decision-making capabilities. Unless marketing makes a special attempt to rectify these conditions, the QOL of these groups are likely to deteriorate.

Large Service Industry Factors

Another aspect of consumer helplessness, as the society becomes more complex, is related to three additional factors: (1) medical services, (2) general service industries, and (3) monopolies. In regard to these three factors, most of the consumers (if not all) cannot cope with their increasing power. Thus, most consumers lose ground in terms of their QOL. These industries' gains come from deteriorating QOLs of large groups of consumers.

Medical Services

Medical services and related industries like health care services and pharmaceutical industries increase in complexity and commensurate cost as the society's complexity evolves. As this book is written, some estimated 35 million Americans have no medical coverage. This is due to increasing medical costs. Medical and related costs have kept ahead of the society's increasing complexity in such a way that some people in our society receive extremely good medical care, while many others do not. In fact, those who receive exceptionally good medical services cost so much to the whole society that the overall cost of medical care is going up for most who receive partial medical care and are not receiving an increasingly improving medical service.

Other Service Industries

Such industries as auto insurance, auto repair, or legal services also are increasing in cost and keeping ahead of the increasing complexity of the society. It appears that both medical services and some other service industries have created a situation in which the consumer's well-being depends on industries' willingness to help. In other words, consumers are at the industries' mercy. Thus, consumers in our markets are not enjoying an equal status as their dependency on these industries continues to increase.

Monopolies

Although many service industries (such as those mentioned in the preceding section) are oligopolistic, they act like a monopoly. These oligopolistic firms are not competing in terms of price and quality; instead, they are competing in terms of promotion and imagery alone. For instance, it is so difficult for consumers to determine real differences among AT&T, MCI, and U.S. Sprint (if any) that a typical consumer hardly can make a rational decision and purchase the best service at the smallest price.

One very distinct monopoly appeared during the writing of this book, the cable TV industry. The cable companies are local monopolies without any control or regulation. They have been raising their rates nonstop and without any explanation to any regulatory agency. Once again, such monopolies hurt those who are not advancing as fast as the society. People who are on fixed incomes and depend upon cable TV for their entertainment have almost no opportunity to go to another similar type of entertainment source.

INADEQUATE INFORMATION

As societal complexity increases, information becomes necessary not to get ahead but simply to cope. There is a consumer information explosion in American markets that is making it more difficult for the four vulnerable groups (minorities, the less educated, the elderly, and the frail).

If one group of consumers does not understand existing information and/or is not able to use it, then the group's chances of optimizing its purchase decisions and purchase behaviors are slim. This situation readily prevails in the four vulnerable consumer groups.

Although there is an information explosion, there is also an information inadequacy. Some information, although critically needed, simply is not available. In other cases, the available information simply muddies the picture and enhances confusion. These situations are particularly prevalent in food-related terms and diets as well as in such over-the-counter drugs as painkillers or headache remedies. There are so many claims and counterclaims that it is almost impossible to comprehend the real picture.

EXCESSIVE SHORT-RUN ORIENTATION

Currently, the American business sector is overwhelmed with the short run. All business activities, all products and services, are expected to yield handsome returns on investment as quickly as possible. The simple outcome of this orientation is suboptimization in the long run. It is maintained here that, as all attempts are geared to maximize short-run activity, suboptimization sets in because many of the short-run decisions are opposed to long-run needs. As American companies emphasize the short run, they deemphasize research and development (R&D), they deemphasize long-term growth, or they deemphasize market development for the long run, and so forth. The outcome of this approach already has been labeled as "stifling" for American industrial growth. If the industry and the economy do not grow, then QOL cannot be improved for all. Once again, the vulnerable groups are likely to be affected adversely.

Feedback on the Deteriorating Quality of Life

Unfortunately, not enough consumers complain. Therefore, consumer complaints are not used as a key source of feedback information regarding the changing QOL. Although there are other such indexes as the consumer outlook index that indicate the degree of optimism or pessimism on the part of consumers, these are not used to determine the overall well-being (or lack thereof) of consumers in our society. The consumer price index (CPI) could be used for such a feedback activity; however, it is not quite accurate in the sense that it does not measure the impact of price changes on different income groups (Samli 1969).

There are other indicators of deteriorating QOL for large groups. The profound increase in the so-called homeless or street people is one such indicator. Over a 20-year period, they have become very noticeable. Occasionally, when certain job openings are advertised, thousands of people will show up for some 20 openings.

These are only a few indicators. There are many others, including some more conventional feedback factors. Market performance is one such broad category. The employment picture, types of jobs available, the characteristics of those who are unemployed, and the nature of newly created jobs are all part of the picture. During the past decade or so, for instance, most of the new jobs have been in the services area and are low paying. Based on this sketchy and unsystematic feedback system, those agencies with the responsibility to protect consumers hardly can perform well.

Agencies of Consumer Protection

Because all consumers are not equal and because some of them need help to take advantage of what our society offers in terms of QOL, there are certain agencies that are in charge of consumer protection. They either perform this task directly by intercepting and correcting certain behaviors that are dangerous or discriminatory, or they perform the task of consumer protection indirectly by trying to improve competition. Four such agencies are discussed briefly here: the Federal Trade Commission (FTC), the Food and Drug Administration (FDA), Offices of Consumer Affairs, and Better Business Bureaus (BBBs).

The FTC explores misleading trade practices and those other practices that may reduce or endanger competition. However, during the past 20 years or so, its powers and its budget have been reduced to a point at which the agency's effectiveness has become rather insignificant.

The FDA is a very critical agency, particularly since there are so many new pharmaceuticals and foodstuffs. However, during the past 20 years this agency has seen some significant budget cuts and an implicit reduction in its responsibilities.

Offices of Consumer Affairs started at the national and state levels around the mid-1960s. They came into being in different states to explore problems related to consumer well-being. Although they sponsored consumer-related legislation, originally this was only one aspect of their overall mission. Around the early 1980s, they became more attached to the offices of state attorney generals. Thus, they lost touch with their original mission of looking after the consumers' well-being in their respective states. They simply became insignificant staff agencies to state offices of the attorney generals.

The three agencies mentioned thus far are government agencies. There are also private agencies that are looking after consumers' well-being. BBBs are such organizations. They are present in every large community. They make sure that competition is legitimate and organizations are not resorting to questionable practices to make a profit. BBBs are important organizations; however, they also suffer the same problems the other public agencies experience. They have limited resources and limited power to enforce certain decisions against questionable business practices. None of the above-mentioned agencies are truly capable of enhancing or at least maintaining current levels of competition.

DECLINING STATE OF COMPETITION

As discussed in Chapters 1–3, competition in the traditional sense is declining in the United States. More and more, oligopolies are taking over different industries and making it virtually impossible for small businesses to enter these industries or to survive. It has been said (but not documented), for instance, that large trucking companies are entering areas where there are small competitors and lowering the rates to a point at which small competitors find it impossible to compete. If and when the small competitor is eliminated, the rates go back up.

Similarly, the current market conditions are such that competitors are being absorbed through unfriendly takeovers or leveraged buyouts. In either case, competition is reduced.

Again, as this book is being written, the number of small businesses entering the market (where they can) is increasing. However, since many of these businesses emerge because the owner cannot find a suitable job elsewhere, they are not necessarily well equipped to cope with the turbulent conditions of the market. Hence, at the point of this writing, the number of business failures in the United States is at an all-time high. The cost of this failure factor (both private and public) is excessive and is taking away the gains of QOL that have been made earlier, just as the cost of the U.S. savings and loan fiasco of the 1990s is shared by the American consumer. In addition, such organizations as the Small Business Administration that help businesses to survive are becoming weaker and/or defunct because of budgetary constraints.

International competition is partially remedying the lessening competition. However, because of international trade deficit problems, international trade is being restricted, which again brings the picture back to lessening competition.

As was pointed out in Chapter 2, when competition deteriorates, the conditions that were envisioned by Adam Smith and his followers are not likely to materialize (Smith 1779). Lessening competition, almost by definition, takes place at the expense of the existing QOL.

SUMMARY

If America is a democracy, consumers in American markets must have equal opportunity to optimize their purchase decisions and purchase behaviors. QOL in America is deteriorating because of ineffective use of resources, increasing societal complexity, inadequate information, excessive short-run orientation, and declining competition. The impact of these factors on consumers is not even. Four groups that are identified as vulnerable are likely to be influenced more adversely than others: minorities, the less educated, the elderly, and the frail. At present, their chances of becoming equal opportunity consumers are deteriorating. There are no direct or indirect forces or agencies to reverse this trend.

APPENDIX
THE ELDERLY AND EQUAL OPPORTUNITY

INTRODUCTION

The elderly portion of society is considered to be the fastest-growing market segment. Not only because of its sheer numbers, but also because of its buying power and unique needs, this market provides great challenges and opportunities for marketing practitioners. However, this group as a whole, just as the frail, minorities, and less educated, does not enjoy equal opportunity consumer status. This appendix explores the status of the elderly and posits proposals as to marketing's social responsibility toward the elderly.

THE GROWTH OF THE OLDER MARKET

Perhaps the most significant change in the consumer markets is the growth of the older population. Individuals over age 65 represented only 10% of the American population in the 1970s. This group is expected to increase to almost 75% of the total population by the year 2050 (*Aging America* 1986). This particular group, although it is not homogeneous, has more varying needs than the society as a whole. Furthermore, this group has a substantially different perspective of life than the rest of the society. Thus, even well-meaning companies that try to provide the society with good products and services cannot satisfy this group's needs. A substantial degree of understanding of the concept of QOL for this group is necessary for businesses to satisfy the needs of this segment and in return be rewarded in terms of high profits. Business needs to be proactive once they understand this segment and its peculiarities (Cooper and Miaoulis 1988). Such authors as Cooper and Miaoulis (1988), in analyzing this group, make a distinction among three types of experiences: (1) the possession experience, (2) the catered experience, and (3) the being experience.

While the *possession experience* describes a basic urge to possess or to own such a specific product as a home or a car. The *catered experience* indicates the satisfaction that is received from such various services as attending a sporting event or going to the theater. The *being experience*, on the other hand, relates to Maslow's self-actualization theory (Wolfe 1987). Individuals in this category receive the highest level of satisfaction from being "fulfilled" individuals who make a real effort to be connected to life. In other words, they appreciate life and little things in it. They value experiences they receive through self-improvement courses or development of interpersonal relationships (Cooper and Miaoulis 1988). Exhibit 4A-1 illustrates marketing's role in all three categories of experiences. Since most companies are not quite in tune with the being experiences of the elderly, almost by definition members of this market segment are not equal opportunity consumers.

The elderly as consumers have special needs, although these needs are not of equal urgency. This is because the elderly are not a homogeneous group. However, most elderly at one time or another experience these special needs. Thus, in order for them to receive the most satisfaction from the being experiences, the elderly need to have their needs met.

Exhibit 4A-1
Experience Satisfaction and Marketing

Experience Category	Description	Marketing's Role
Possession Experience	Ownership of products such as cars, home, etc.	Provide products that are satisfying the needs for tangible goods.
Catered Experiences	Favoring travel, theater, sports events, other less tangible, more service-oriented products and services.	Provide services that are satisfactory and products with important service components.
Being Experiences	Focus more on the sense of being associated with life and satisfaction with joys of living.	Provide products and services indicates clearly understanding of the elderly consumer's needs and enhance their quality of life.

What are the elderly's special needs? How could marketing satisfy these needs so that the elderly may become equal opportunity consumers? It must be realized that the older segment's ability to become equal opportunity consumers and to participate in the marketplace as such is seen to increase this segment's importance and to provide countless opportunities for marketing practitioners (Sherman 1989). However, it is equally important to note that, if properly constructed, marketing activities can enhance life satisfaction (Sherman and Cooper 1988). Life satisfaction is related to "one's ability to maintain an optimistic outlook, to find life pleasurable and to hold a positive sense of self" (Balars and Schewe 1989, 255). No matter how vital in physical and mental health, the elderly experience home restrictions in their social and economic lives that cause numerous other problems for them as consumers. These problems make them less-than-equal opportunity consumers. Among these problems are (1) relationship problems, (2) need for special products, (3) need for special services, (4) information needs, and (5) economic problems.

1. *Relationship Problems.* The family, work, and other social relationships start becoming problematic as the individual ages. Transitions take place in these areas in such a way that individuals find themselves with reversed roles or no roles at all. They also become more and more lonely and left out. Sherman suggests that: "Reference groups change that accompanies aging has been accommodated for by the sprouting up of many varied social outlets that promote new social interactions" (1989, 260).

Activities centers, senior travel clubs, and senior center associations can be considered as proactive marketing groups.

2. *Need for Special Products.* As they get older, the elderly need different products. The product needs vary from special foods to special apparel and to specially designed homes and furniture. In addition to their unique needs and products specifically designed and marketed for these needs, the elderly purchase a lot of products for others. They buy a large proportion of toys for children. They also buy large numbers of various gifts and other products not for their own use but for use by others. It is therefore important to communicate with this sector effectively in addition to generating specific products that will satisfy the needs of the elderly.

3. *Need for Special Services.* The elderly need many different types of services. First, perhaps one of the most critical types of service is related to self-image. Projecting realistic, positive images of the older couple is a necessity to improve the elderly's QOL (Dychtwald 1989). This implies that certain services that will provide an opportunity for the elderly to make a contribution to the society and reinstate self-worth are necessary. Certain volunteer services, charitable organizations, and promotional activities displaying the elderly and their contribution to the society in a positive context are to be generated.

The second group of services is related to medical and health care. The elderly's medical and health care needs are rather different and in some cases more intensified. Marketing must find ways to generate and deliver appropriate services at reasonable costs for these particular consumers. In this case, the service quality considerations become particularly critical. Thus, marketing has to monitor the quality carefully. In this context, one area particularly stands out, that of nursing home marketing (Davis 1989). This very important area is still in its infancy. Much needs to be done to establish quality and cost and associate the two for an efficient and effective service that is likely to have a spectacular growth market (Davis 1989).

4. *Information Needs.* Because the elderly are quite attached to their routines and certain ways of performing life functions, communicating with them is not a simple process. Part of their communication is related to their particular reference groups, the behavior and interaction of which influence the elderly. Among these reference groups are siblings, friends, neighbors, and service providers (Sherman 1989). These cohort groups carry a major role in communicating with the elderly. However, these groups, in time, change, disappear, or are replaced by others. Mass-media exposure of the elderly also is different. Marketing must make good use of special media to which the elderly are exposed. This will enable the discipline to communicate effectively with this segment. Marketing needs to be

in touch with the elderly, particularly to inform them about different product and service options and to help them to stay informed so that they can make good purchase decisions.

5. *Economic Problems.* Although the elderly may have substantial wealth accumulated, their incomes, quite often, are limited (Lazer and Shaw, 1989). Marketing, in order to gain the broadest possible reach to this segment and the most intensified cultivation of it, must generate reasonably priced products and services. It also must find creative ways of financing the older consumers' purchases.

OPERATIONALIZING THE ENHANCEMENT OF EQUAL OPPORTUNITY

The five areas discussed above are critical for the elderly market. Marketing, by catering to this segment's needs and by helping it to cope with these problem areas, will enhance the QOL of the elderly as a group while also experiencing desirable profits. Although marketing's challenge is formidable in improving the elderly's status as equal opportunity consumers, marketing's profit opportunities are equally formidable.

Exhibit 4A-1 presents a model by which marketing can face the challenge of serving the elderly market segment. The model posits that understanding the particular needs of this segment is the most important first step. It leads to development of unique and suitable products and services for this segment. The model emphasizes the importance of communication with this group. Furthermore, the model brings into focus that market penetration is the way to equal opportunity enhancement.

Finally, Exhibit 4A-2 brings about one of the most important areas in marketing to this group, feedback. Because of its many unique characteristics, the elderly market is particularly vulnerable and feedback followed by corrective action is extremely important. There needs to be research as to how feedback systems can be established to monitor marketing's performance.

SUMMARY

This appendix explores how marketing can help improve the elderly's position as equal opportunity consumers. Marketing's role in this case is formidable but also very rewarding. Similar models need to be developed for other unique market segments so that an enhancement in the equal opportunity consumer status of all consumers in our society can be achieved.

Exhibit 4A-2
Marketing's Functions to Improve the Elderly's Position as
Equal Opportunity Consumers

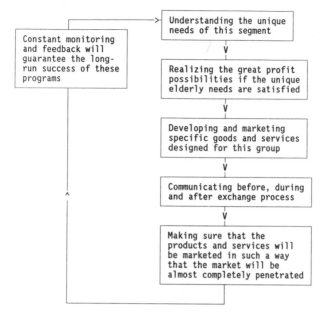

REFERENCES

Aging America: Trends and Projections 1985–1986 Edition. 1986. Washington, DC: U.S. Government Printing Office, 1986.

Balars, Anne L., and Charles D. Schewe. 1989. "The Impact of Changing Roles on the Mature Consumer." In *Quality-of-Life Studies in Marketing and Management*, edited by H. Lee Meadow and M. Joseph Sirgy, 254–264. Blacksburg, VA: Virginia Tech.

Cooper, Philip D., and George Miaoulis. 1988. "Altering Corporate Strategic Criteria to Reflect the Changing Environment: The Role of Life Satisfaction and the Growing Senior Market." *California Management Review* (Fall):87–97.

Davis, Mark A. 1989. "Establishing the Link between Nursing Home Costs and Nursing Home Quality." In *Quality-of-Life Studies in Marketing and Management*, edited by H. Lee Meadow and M. Joseph Sirgy, 280–290. Blacksburg, VA: Virginia Tech.

Dychtwald, Ken. 1989. *Age Wave: The Challenges and Opportunities of an Aging America*. Los Angeles: Jeremy P. Tarcher, Inc.

Kennedy, John F. 1963. "Consumer Advisory Council: First Report." Executive Office of the President, Washington, DC: United States Government Printing Office, October.

Lazer, William, and Eric H. Shaw. 1989. "Income, Assets and Consumption: The Relative Well Being of Mature Consumers." In *Quality-of-Life Studies in Marketing and Management*, edited by H. Lee Meadow and M. Joseph Sirgy, 265–279. Blacksburg, VA: Virginia Tech.

Naisbitt, John. 1982. *Megatrends*. New York: Warner Books.

Samli, A. Coskun. 1969. "Differential Price Structures for the Rich and the Poor." *University of Washington Business Review* (Summer):36–43.

Sherman, Elaine. 1989. "A Retrospective of Selected Issues Concerning Quality of Life and the Elderly Consumer." In *Quality-of-Life Studies in Marketing and Management*, edited by H. Lee Meadow and M. Joseph Sirgy, 228–238. Blacksburg, VA: Virginia Tech.

Sherman, Elaine, and Philip Cooper. 1988. "Life Satisfaction: The Missing Focus of Marketing to Seniors." *Journal of Health Care Marketing* (March):69–71.

Smith, Adam. 1779. *Wealth of Nations*. London: George Routledge.

Spratlin, Thaddeus H. 1991. "The Controversy Over Targeting Black Consumers in Cigarette Advertising, Racial/Ethnic and Ethical Issues." In *Developments in Marketing Science*, Vol. 14, edited by Robert L. King, 249–253. Miami: Academy of Marketing Science.

Strutton, David, and R. Keith Tudor. 1991. "A Conceptually Based Discussion of Possible Antecedents and Social Implications Associated with Marketing's Stereotypical Portrayal of Blacks." In *Developments in Marketing Science*, Vol. 14, edited by Robert L. King, 245–248. Miami: Academy of Marketing Science.

Wolfe, D. B. 1987. "Marketing to the Ageless Market: Seniors." *American Demographics* (July):26–30.

5 | Distorted Risk Management as It Affects Underprivileged Consumers

A. Coskun Samli, Mary Ann Lederhaus, and M. Joseph Sirgy

If one were to digress from the classical economists' position that consumers are all optimizers and rational economic creatures and move in the direction of behaviorists, then a major problem stems from the fact that individuals have different mental capabilities, different levels of education, and different perceptive systems. If, for the reasons of mental incapability, lack of education, or distorted perception system, one were to receive distorted risk messages and as a consumer try to manage this distorted risk, what would be some of the consequences? It is posited in this chapter that the outcome of attempts to optimize under distorted perceived risk conditions will suboptimize the effectiveness of consumers' decisions. As the result of this suboptimization, the overall quality of life (QOL) will be suboptimized. Thus, unless this situation is rectified, the society's overall loss will grow commensurate to the size and overall economic power of these three groups.

How could the individuals be helped to eliminate the distortion in the risk perception and/or how can they be helped to manage the distorted risk more effectively? The problems of related distorted risk management are likely to be accentuated if the subjects are members of the underprivileged group in our society.

INTRODUCTION

Perhaps the oldest science dealing with individuals' purchasing-behavior patterns is economics. The core assumption in classical economics is that the consumer is an all-knowing and calculating creature (Samuelson 1972) who attempts to maximize utilities in purchasing. Such new social sciences as consumer behavior and social psychology have advanced the notion, however, that individuals are differently endowed and may not necessarily maximize utilities in their purchases (Engel, Blackwell, and Miniard 1990). Consumers tend to establish a purchasing norm that may be consistent with either of the above notions, and deviations from the established purchasing notion may inhibit satisfaction and lead to a number of such problems as discrepant behavior, thwarted expectancy, and even cognitive dissonance (Engel, Kollat, and Blackwell 1978; Howard and Sheth 1969; Festinger 1957).

The purpose of this chapter is to attempt to establish a closer link between the economists' point of view and that of the behaviorist by looking at how distorted risk management, as defined in the next section, affects underprivileged consumers. Marketing and public policy solutions to the problem are explored and articulated.

Approximately one-fifth of American society is composed of consumers who are considered to live below poverty lines. They are not well equipped to make good purchase decisions to optimize their satisfaction as consumers. Furthermore, various mass media estimate that around 25% of our society is labeled as "functional illiterates," which implies inability to follow written instructions. Functional illiterates are in an even worse position than those who are below the poverty line. They cannot read and calculate best buys even though they may need to make such decisions. If the average IQ (intelligence quotient) is 100, then, by definition, one-half of the American population has an IQ below 100.

Because of the overlapping effect of components, we find that a large number of American consumers are underprivileged in that they do not possess the funds, educational achievement, or mental capability to be knowledgeable and calculating people who are capable of maximizing their utilities in purchasing. In this chapter, members of the underprivileged group are termed "frail" consumers. *Frail consumers* are conceptualized as those consumers who not only cannot optimize purchase satisfaction but, also, because of distorted risk management, become even more underprivileged. Frailty leads to less satisfaction in the purchase of products and services. Thus, there is a circular snowballing effect that is worsening this group's QOL.

Exhibit 5-1 conceptualizes the progression leading to consumer frailty. Inspection of the illustration indicates that the mediating element is distorted risk management, which leads to frailty. Consumer frailties tend to exist because such inhibiting conditions as low socioeconomic levels, immobility, limited analytical and risk-coping skills, poor risk perception, and poor risk reduction are present. As seen in Exhibit 5-1, this situation is self-perpetuating. Underprivileged consumers with the accentuating factors are per-

Exhibit 5-1
Self-Perpetuating Consumer Frailty

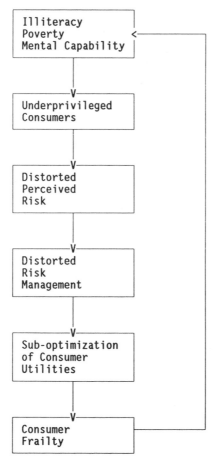

ceiving distorted risks, which leads to distorted risk management. Distorted risk management leads to suboptimization of consumer utilities. This further exacerbates the frailness of these consumers. The situation is circular and not self-correcting. Thus, the larger the number of frail consumers, the greater is the social loss in terms of foregone consumer satisfaction. However, there also are very large marketing losses in terms of lost profits from many meaningful products and services that would be purchased if the frail consumers were to get out of the frailty syndrome and revert to average and normal risk managers.

DISTORTED RISK MANAGEMENT

All consumers have certain risk perceptions and all consumers somehow behave in such a way that their perceived risk will be managed (Schiffman and Kanuk 1990). For example, perceptions of risk could result from uncertainty about the brand or product as well as the severity or importance of negative consequences associated with product failure (Bauer 1967; Tarpey and Peter 1975). Risk management implies that consumers could follow one of two courses — that is, risk avoidance management on the basis of prepurchase decisions or postpurchase risk management. For instance, risk avoidance behavior can manifest itself simply through such prepurchase decisions as extensive searching for information or a degree of brand loyalty that precludes the entrance of new brands into the evoked set or selection of alternatives. Postpurchase risk management occurs on the basis of after-purchase decisions and the process a consumer goes through in evaluating the appropriateness of the alternative chosen. If risks are not managed, however, they then can become distorted and, as discussed in this chapter, risk-reduction techniques will fail to work.

RISK AVOIDANCE/RISK MANAGEMENT

The literature is rich in its treatment of the notion of consumer frailties from decision-making, information-processing, and economic theory points of view. It falls short in the treatment of the subject from a risk management point of view.

Bauer concludes that consumer behavior "involves risk in the sense that any action of a consumer will produce consequences which he cannot anticipate with anything approximating certainty, and some of which at least are likely to be unpleasant" (1967, 390). The perception of risk in a purchase situation, therefore, becomes a function of uncertainty as well as possible negative consequences. The degree of consumer-perceived risk and the consumer's own tolerance for risk taking serve to influence purchase strategies.

Frail consumers do not seem to have the same type of risk-perception and tolerance-for-risk capabilities that other consumers may have, however, because of the frail consumers' underprivileged nature. This tends to lead to distorted risk perception and subsequent distorted risk management. The five examples that follow describe this process.

First, non-English-speaking Latino consumers may have totally exaggerated perceptions of a store manager who does not speak English. Hence, the Latino may feel that the store manager will take advantage of him or her.

Second, it is almost an impossibility for the undereducated to calculate the best buy as reflected by unit pricing. In many cases, unit pricing may not be readily available. If it is available, it may necessitate some basic calculations by consumers, especially when weight comparisons are dissimilar, such as one product using pounds and another using ounces as units of measure. Unit pricing also may require that consumers use certain types of reasoning to compare the quality and price combinations to arrive at the best choice in a retail outlet.

Third, for a person with slightly less than average intelligence, it may be impossible to calculate the loan, interest rates, and obligations of the buyer in the case of such a complicated purchase activity as buying a car or a house.

Fourth, any of these conditions or any combination is likely to disable the consumer from seeing the risk involved in a purchase transaction or may force the consumer to misunderstand the risk involved. The person, for instance, may need to go to the dentist but prefers to buy a Nintendo or an Atari game instead.

Fifth, for a person lacking opportunity for an education, owning and mastering the use of a personal computer (PC), for example, approaches an impossibility. Furthermore, if that person was to have access to this piece of equipment, he or she may not be able to determine how to use or how to care for the equipment.

Risk may arise from any of the following factors (Jacoby and

Kaplan 1972; Zigmund and Scott 1973; Ferber and Lee 1974; Locander and Herman 1979; Roselius 1971):

- Performance: Risk that the product will not perform as expected.
- Financial: Risk that the product will be worth less than its cost in money.
- Physical: Risk that the product may pose to the self and to others.
- Social: Risk of embarrassment before others because of poor product choice.
- Psychological: Risk of ego degradation because of poor product choice.

Social and psychological risks are highly dependent upon consumers' personal and subjective factors, and establishing norms for consumer behavior related to these risks is very difficult. The performance, financial, and physical risks, however, can be analyzed by less-subjective means, thereby allowing behavioral norms associated with these risks to be established. For the purposes of this chapter, performance, financial, and physical risk are referred to as *functional* risks (as opposed to social or psychological). Functional risks may give rise to consumer frailties if risk perceptions are highly discrepant. Because of their objective nature, these three dimensions may be assessed by using some means of gathering information about the product prior to purchase. As mentioned in the section, "Distorted Risk Management," risk avoidance can occur through the acquisition of information about a product. For example, ratings given by *Consumer Reports*, which uses a consensus of consumer experts, suggest that one source for a particular product would yield risk avoidance, but this source of information generally is not available to the underprivileged.

Consumers generally are faced with two types of purchase uncertainties. One uncertainty pertains to the predicted consequences of selecting a particular alternative, and the other pertains to the extent to which each possible consequence of this alternative will contribute to, or detract from, a resolution to the problem (Humphreys and Kenderdine 1979). Taylor (1974) refers to these two dimensions of uncertainty as "uncertainty about consequence" and "uncertainty about outcome," respectively, both of which may be alleviated by acquiring and using information to reduce negative consequences. For example, a consumer buys a bottle of wine and is uncertain that the wine will complement fish (uncertainty about outcome). Furthermore, the consumer is fearful that the wine may be spoiled (uncertainty about consequence) and would wish not to serve it with dinner. These uncertainties can be alleviated by obtaining and using relevant information to help reduce the negative consequences of a poor decision. They also point to the importance of policies pertaining to the dissemination of quality, value-oriented marketing information for consumer processing.

From a marketing policy standpoint, then, risk management strategies may reflect tendencies to buy brands (1) endorsed by celebrities or experts (testimonials), (2) with which the consumer has been satisfied in the past (brand loyalty), (3) that are well known (major brand image), (4) tested and approved by a private testing company (*Consumer Reports, Good Housekeeping*, Underwriter Laboratories), (5) carried by a store that is perceived to be dependable and reputable (store image), (6) used on a trial basis before buying (free samples), (7) offering a money-back guarantee, (8) tested and approved by the government (especially the Food and Drug Administration [FDA]), (9) on which product features on several brands in several stores have been compared (comparative shopping), (10) on which advice about the product from family and friends has been received (word of mouth), (11) on which brand names clearly describe the product (brand reputation), and (12) last, but not least, on which reputations become well established (delayed adoption) (Bettman 1972, 1973; Roselius 1971; Schiffman and Kanuk 1990). Relevant information about each of these risk relievers to reduce differential amounts of risk generally is not gathered by the underprivileged, however. It should be pointed out that different consumers use different risk relievers, depending upon the circumstances involved. The underprivileged consumer simply may use past satisfaction and ease of purchase as judging criteria. Lack of English fluency and/or reasoning abilities may preclude other alternatives. For example, Reece and Ducoff (1987) studied the meanings of key words used in brand names and how these key words caused misunderstandings among consumers. Misunderstanding of such words as "plus" may not come strictly from advertising but also may come from the brand names themselves (Lazarus 1985). Loken, Ross, and Hinkle (1986) showed in results of a laboratory study that similarities in appearance of two brands, such as a national brand and a private-label brand, may cause confusion.

Private-label products often were perceived as having the same origin as national brands.

In order better to understand dilemmas that face consumers in making decisions, a discussion of functional risk is presented next.

Functional Risk Construct Operationalization

For our purposes, performance, financial, and physical risks, in contrast to social and psychological risks, are referred to as functional risks. Perceptions of functional risk result from such factors as uncertainty about the functional nature of a product or the severity or importance of possible negative consequences associated with product failure (Peter and Ryan 1976).

Adhering to Peter and Ryan's expectancy-value formulation involving the relationship between brand preference and risk perception,[1] functional risk perception *PST* for a given consumer for a brand can be represented as the average sum of the uncertainty strength *U* and the magnitude of the negative consequence *N* components for each of the functional risk components: performance *P*, financial *F*, and physical *H* risks.[2] This relationship can be represented mathematically as

$$PST_k = \left(\sum_{i=2}^{I} PSP_{ik} \right) W_p + \left(\sum_{e=1}^{E} PSF_{ek} \right) W_f$$

$$+ \left(\sum_{j=2}^{J} PSH_{jk} \right) W_h \ldots \tag{5-1}$$

where

PST_k = Perceived functional risk for a given consumer k for a given brand

PSP_{ik} = $UP_{ik}NP_{ik}$, where UP_{ik} = uncertainty about negative performance consequence i, and NP_{ik} = magnitude of negative performance consequence i associated with the purchase and/or usage of that brand for consumer k

PSF_{ek} = $UF_{ek}NF_{ek}$, where UF_{ek} = uncertainty about negative financial consequence e and NF_{ek} = magnitude of negative financial consequence e associated with the purchase and/or usage of that brand for consumer k

$PSH_{jk} = UH_{jk}NH_{jk}$, where UH_{jk} = uncertainty about negative physical consequences j, and NH_{jk} = magnitude of negative physical consequence j associated with the purchase and/or usage of that brand for consumer k

W_p, W_f, W_h = parameter weights

For example, using the ratings of *Consumer Reports*, a sample of informed consumers can be instructed to study attributes of a particular product and, in turn, rate this product along the three risk dimensions extrapolated in the formula. The risk measures will generate a type of quasi-objective ratings for the product. From these ratings, then, mean objective functional risk scores POT and standard deviations $_{POT}$ can be generated. Similarly, means and standard deviations for the objective ratings pertaining to the three functional-risk components POP, POF, and POH can be obtained. A significant positive or negative deviation between the perceived functional risk and the objective functional risk could cause distorted risk management and lead to consumer frailty. This can be represented mathematically through the use of a Z-formula:

$$PT_k = (PST_k - POT)/_{POT} \qquad (5\text{-}2)$$

where

PT_k = the functional risk deviation score of consumer k regarding a particular brand

If $PT_k > 1$ then $PST_k = HPST_k$ (high risk perception misconception). If $PT_k < 1$ then $PST_k = LPST_k$ (low risk perception misconception).

Similarly, high and low risk perception misconception can be detected for the three functional risk components P, F, and H. In this way, if a consumer's risk perception is found to be significantly discrepant from the so-called objective rating, it can be said that the consumer has distorted risk perception.

OPTIMAL BEHAVIOR ILLUSTRATED

Risk management methods to reduce risk have been addressed robustly in the literature and include information search, brand loyalty, selection by brand or store popularity, and selection by price, among other methods. Almost all consumers seem to have a basic risk-reduction mechanism that they habitually use. This mechanism, however, may fail to function properly if the original risk is misperceived because of a consumer's frailties. As mentioned in the section, "Distorted Risk Management," poorly managed risk leads to risk distortion.

One key behavior to the avoidance of distorted risk management is an expanded information search process. It would help reduce misperceptions arising from potential unfamiliarity with a product that arise when a significant deviation from present familiarity to an optimal familiarity occurs. Again, the optimal familiarity could be established by using *Consumer Reports* or a consensus of experts. Expanding this notion allows construction of a semantic differential instrument in which *Consumer Reports* ratings can be translated into a set of performance, financial, and physical impact bipolar adjectives. Products then can be rated along their functional characteristics using the semantic differential scale. Optimal mean ratings Olm and standard deviations $_{Olm}$ for each attribute m can be calculated using the same formula developed in Eq. 5-2 above. A consumer's actual familiarity (see Sirgy 1981 for a theoretical exposition of product familiarity in consumer research) with product attributes can yield a functional familiarity score Slm. This Z-formula score then can be compared with the optimal Olm:

$$IM_k = (Slm_k - \overline{Olm})/_{Olm} \qquad (5\text{-}3)$$

where

IM = the deviation score of a given consumer k's familiarity with functional attribute m from optimal familiarity for a given product

If $IM_k > \pm 1$ then $Slm_k = FSlm_k$, where $FSlm_k$ = nonoptimal functional risk familiarity.

Of course, the formula does not have to be restricted to detecting and measuring unfamiliarity. For example, data can be generated for studying brand loyalty, brand and store popularity, and price quality. In each case, the Z-formula allows a comparison of the construct under study with an optimal score. The closer the frail consumer can move toward the optimal score, the greater is the degree of positive risk management that will occur.

PROPOSED CORRECTIVE ACTION

It is quite apparent that the consumer frailty concept defined and presented in this chapter pertains to consumption behavior of the underprivileged and undercompetent. The chapter presents a proposed perspective on how risk management that becomes distorted affects a consumer and how distorted risk management might develop in the absence of guidance, education, information, and/or protection.

Corrective action can come in three different forms: consumer education, consumer information, and consumer protection. Consumer education programs designed to increase awareness are emerging, but consumer advocates and policy makers need to make sure that means are developed to disseminate this information to the underprivileged.

Distorted risk management can be exacerbated by not obtaining and using relevant information to help reduce the negative consequences of a poor decision. The importance of policies pertaining to the dissemination of quality, value-oriented marketing information for consumer processing cannot be stressed enough. The means through which these policies can be achieved can take many forms, including (1) comparative testing as done by *Consumer Reports*, (2) such informative labeling as clearly written, descriptive labels found on many products (note that larger, sans serif print will make reading descriptive labels easier for older adults or those with visual impairments), (3) quality certification by the U.S. Department of Agriculture (USDA) and the FDA, (4) such formal consumer advice centers as the Better Business Bureau (BBB), local churches, or any other location where underprivileged consumers can be concentrated. The knowledge derived from the programs described above can help to alleviate the severity of consumer frailties and allow the presently underprivileged consumer to perform a more significant role in the free marketplace by increasing the likelihood that he or she will be able to manage purchase decisions. In addition, the same proposed perspective can be used to examine the impact of distorted risk management on such variables as sales volume, market share, price levels, market concentration, and barriers to entry.

Consumer protection is essential, particularly to protect those who are not quite capable of making optimal decisions. These people may be more susceptible to certain dangerous products, environmentally unfriendly products, or economically undesirable products. Consumer protection therefore may vary from banning certain products such as Red Dye No. 2 to specifying certain trade practices such as truth in lending. Additional protection may be provided for those who appear to be more frail in general or more vulnerable to negative effects of certain products (Sirgy and Samli 1988).

SUMMARY

Explaining, predicting, and controlling distorted risk management as it affects underprivileged consumers and leads to frailties appears to be a legitimate topic that may contribute to both marketing and consumer affairs policy decisions. An attempt, therefore, has been made to provide marketers and policy makers with a conceptual framework from which the frail consumer and distorted risk management can be investigated.

Based on economic theory, risk management, by definition, implies an informed consumer whose rational decisions in the market place become important in preserving the full integrity of society and the free-enterprise system. Some consumers, because of their social and innate endowments, are more effective than others in reacting to and coping with their environments. Other consumers, more specifically the frail, underprivileged consumers, are less able to avail themselves of information sources or to differentiate reliable from unreliable products. They are unable to differentiate between deceptive and nondeceptive advertising, are usually brand loyal because of an inherent inability to search for substitutes, and are unable to make price and quality judgments about products and services because of physical and geographical immobility.

In conclusion, risk management may be investigated from the perspective that distortions in the risk management process are a direct function of consumer-related and situation-related as well as consumer-situation interaction-related factors. Further investigation into risk management as it mediates consumer frailties is needed. Additional forms of risk management techniques need to be defined conceptually and operationalized. Perhaps the most important contribution of this chapter is that it recognizes that distorted risk management as it affects underprivileged consumers is a somewhat neglected area of research and that the concepts extrapolated here pave the way for future consumer studies.

NOTES

1. Peter and Ryan (1976) used expectancy-value formulation popular in multiattribute attitude models in relating perceived risk to brand preference or purchase choice. They argued that a consumer's brand preference BP_k can be construed as an inverse function of the sum of the probability of losses or certainty of negative consequence PL_{ik}, or the sum of the product of the probability of the loss and the importance of that loss across all evoked losses $PL_{ik}PI_{ik}$. Therefore

$$BP_k = \text{inverse function } PL_{ik} \quad \text{or}$$
$$BP_k = \text{inverse function } PL_{ik}PI_{ik}$$

However, since we only are interested in the perceived risk construct and not the brand preference construct, perceived risk can be construed as a multiplicative function of the inverse of the probability of loss PL_{ik} and the importance of that loss PI_{ik}.

2. However, these subjective ratings should not be performed without controlling for the frame-of-reference or comparative set. From the social cognition literature, we know that evaluations usually are made in comparison to an "evoked criterion," "standard," "frame of reference," "comparison set," and so on (Wyer and Carlston 1978; Nisbett and Ross 1981). Therefore, a paired comparison procedure is recommended here. A number of brands within the same product category are compared between and among themselves in a paired comparison format.

REFERENCES

Bauer, Raymond A. 1967. "Consumer Behavior as Risk Taking." In *Risk Taking and Information Handling in Consumer Behavior*, edited by Donald F. Cox, 23–33. Boston: Division of Research, Graduate School of Business Administration, Harvard University.

Bettman, James R. 1972. "Perceived Risk: A Measurement Methodology and Preliminary Findings." In *Proceedings of the Third Annual Conference of the Association for Consumer Research*, edited by M. Venkatesan, 394–403. Association for Consumer Research.

Bettman, James R. 1973. "Perceived Risk and Its Components: Model and Empirical Test." *Journal of Marketing Research* 10:184–190.

Engel, James, Roger D. Blackwell, and Paul W. Miniard. 1990. *Consumer Behavior*, 5th ed. New York: CBS College Publishing.

Engel, James F., David T. Kollat, and Roger D. Blackwell. 1978. *Consumer Behavior*, 2d ed. New York: The Dryden Press.

Ferber, Robert, and Lucy Chao Lee. 1974. "Husband-Wife Influence in Family Purchasing Behavior." *Journal of Consumer Research* 1 (June):43–50.

Festinger, Leon. 1957. *A Theory of Cognitive Dissonance*. Stanford, CA: Stanford University Press.

Howard, John, and Jagdish Sheth. 1969. *The Theory of Buyer Behavior*. New York: John Wiley and Sons.

Humphreys, M. A., and J. M. Kenderdine. 1979. "They've Even Made Him to Lawyers." Norman, OK: Working Paper Series No. 78-7, University of Oklahoma, Division of Marketing.

Jacoby, J., and L. B. Kaplan. 1972. "The Components of Perceived Risk." *Proceedings of the Third Annual Conference of the Association for Consumer Research* 382–93.

Jakoby, J., and D. B. Kyner. 1973. "Brand Loyalty versus Repeat Purchase Behavior." *Journal of Marketing Research* 10:1–9.

Lazarus, George. 1985. "'Plus' is a Minus These Days." *Adweek* (October 28):8.

Locander, W. B., and P. W. Herman. 1979. "The Effect of Self-Confidence and Anxiety on Information Seeking in Consumer Risk Reduction." *Journal of Marketing Research* 16:268–274.

Loken, Barbara, Ivan Ross, and Ronald L. Hinkle. 1986. "Consumer 'Confusion' of Origin and Brand Similarity Perceptions." *Journal of Public Policy and Marketing* 5:195–211.

Nisbett, R., and L. Ross. 1981. *Human Inference: Strategies and Shortcomings of Social Judgments*. Englewood Cliffs, NJ: Prentice-Hall.

Peter, J. Paul, and Michael J. Ryan. 1976. "An Investigation of Perceived Risk at the Brand Level." *Journal of Marketing Research* 13:184–189.

Reece, Bonnie B., and Robert H. Ducoff. 1987. "Deception in Brand Names." *Journal of Public Policy and Marketing* 6:93–103.

Roselius, T. 1971. "Consumer Rankings of Risk Reduction Methods." *Journal of Marketing* 35:56–61.

Samuelson, Paul A. 1972. *Economics*, 9th ed. New York: McGraw-Hill Book Company.

Schiffman, Leon G., and Leslie L. Kanuk. 1990. *Consumer Behavior*, 3d ed. Englewood Cliffs, NJ: Prentice-Hall.

Sirgy, M. Joseph. 1981. "Product Familiarity: Critical Comments on Selected Studies and Theoretical Extensions." In *Advances in Consumer Research*, Vol. 8, edited by Kent Monroe. Ann Arbor, MI: Association for Consumer Research.

Sirgy, M. Joseph, and A. Coskun Samli. 1988. "Functional/Dysfunctional Consumer Behavior: A Normative Framework for Public Policy." In *Minority Marketing*, edited by R. L. King, 78–82. Charleston, SC: Academy of Marketing Science.

Tarpey, Lawrence X., Sr., and J. Paul Peter. 1975. "A Comparative Analysis of Three Consumer Decision Strategies." *Journal of Consumer Research* 2:29–37.

Taylor, James W. 1974. "The Role of Risk in Consumer Behavior." *Journal of Marketing* 38(2):54–60.

Wyer, R. S., Jr., and D. E. Carlston. 1978. *Social Cognition, Inference, and Attribution*. Hillsdale, NJ: Erlbaum.

Zikmund, W. G., and J. E. Scott. 1973. "A Multivariate Analysis of Perceived Risk, Self-Confidence, and Information Sources." In *Advances in Consumer Research*, Vol. 1, edited by Scott Ward and Peter Wright. Ann Arbor, MI: Association for Consumer Research.

6 | Why Ethics Do Not Work

One may think that if the corporate entity were to follow a certain ethical path of behavior, then there would be no reason for the three corrective actions—consumer education, consumer information, and consumer protection—raised in Chapter 5. After all, if ethical behavior means responsible behavior, then the individual firm will do what is proper. Indeed, many who have faith in the market system suggest that if there were no regulations and government interferences, all businesses would act ethically and competition would take care of everything. The competition part of this argument is examined in Chapters 1–3. It has been observed that competition is decreasing and there are pathological conditions. Therefore, left alone, the market will not produce the results that could have been expected in Adam Smith's market (Smith 1779). In this chapter, we examine the second part of the premise that businesses are ethical and left alone will do the proper things for themselves and the market.

DIFFERING OPINIONS ABOUT ETHICS

As Cullen, Victor, and Stephens pointed out, "there is no shortage of differing opinions about what businesses should do in various situations and about what constitutes ethical behavior" (1989, 50). They give the following case as an illustration of ethical behavior:

In 1982 and again in 1986, grisly reports of poisoning by tainted Tylenol hit the newsstands. Within hours of hearing of the crisis, McNeil Laboratories, a subsidiary of Johnson and Johnson, voluntarily and completely withdrew the product from the market—and this in spite of the fact that the disaster resulted from tampering rather than manufacturing error. The *Washington Post* described the company's efforts as a textbook example of a firm's willingness to do what is right, regardless of cost. Why did McNeil make the decision that it did? The often cited response was, "It's the J&J way."

Without taking away any credit from Johnson and Johnson, what they did was the best marketing move under the circumstances. Instead of risking a major shake-up in the consumers' trust toward Tylenol™, the company used the circumstances as a promotional device indicating how "careful" and "caring" the company really is. In this particular situation, perhaps the most appropriate ethical stance was also the most appropriate marketing move. However, one may wonder under what circumstances the most appropriate marketing decision would overlap with the most reasonable ethical position. Good ethics, just as in this case, may ensure good profits, although good ethicists maintain that those companies that are "ethical" because that is the profitable posture are being ethical for the wrong reason ("Do Good Ethics Ensure Good Profits?" 1989). They are not being quite realistic. Businesses need to survive first. If survival and being ethical are not perceived by the decision maker to be very closely related, then the decision maker is likely to opt to make money regardless of ethical consequences. This creates a serious problem for the consumer as well as the society.

MARKETING AND ETHICS RELATIONSHIPS

Perhaps comparing the relationships between marketing and ethics will shed some light on the profitability considerations. Although being ethical for the sake of being ethical is an admirable goal, it must be remembered that businesses are in existence to make money. When it is speculated that "if, as a consequence (of being ethical) its profits are reduced (of a particular business), it must accept such a trade-off without regret" ("Do Good Ethics Ensure Good Profits?" 4), in practice, this may be quite an impossibility. Consider, for instance, a furniture store where business has been very poor. The owner in sheer desperation sets the store on fire to collect insurance. In such situations of extreme hardship or pressure, business may not be considering ethical behavior as a first choice. Survival is always the highest priority and, in order to achieve it, that particular business may forego, partially or fully, its ethical stance.

Because the current American market is quite far removed from perfect competition, the market does not necessarily reward good ethical behavior. Exhibit 6-1 illustrates marketing and ethical behavior relationships. As was seen in the case of Tylenol, good marketing and good ethical behavior prove to be highly profitable. It is not necessary to question which came first; it only must be realized that there is a high degree of correlation between ethical behavior and good marketing that leads to a high level of profitability. If the market is perfectly competitive, then ethical behavior is necessary for business survival. However, since the present American market is far from Adam Smith's market, ethical behavior is not an inseparable part of successful business behavior.

The lower-left quadrant of Exhibit 6-1 illustrates that good marketing without good ethics is possible and it may even pay. The further away the market is from perfect competition, the more feasible it becomes to develop effective marketing plans without considering good ethics. Many direct mail, telemarketing, and other direct marketing practices are accused of being in this category. This is not to accuse the whole industry, rather to point out that some unethical marketing practices may work and may be quite profitable.

The upper-right quadrant of Exhibit 6-1 illustrates good ethical

Exhibit 6-1
Marketing and Ethics Relationships

	Good Marketing	Poor Marketing
Good Ethics	Most profitable and satisfactory	Borderline profitability
Poor Ethics	Still profitable	Losing proposition

behavior with poor (or ineffective) marketing practices. To the extent that the market is somewhat competitive and to the extent that the firm's ethical stance is well known and appreciated, that firm can manage to survive. Consider, for instance, a local plumber known for honesty (justifiably), who has been doing very little advertising and other necessary marketing functions to make his or her business a success. However, because his or her honesty is well known, a certain group of satisfied customers and others who are influenced by these customers can help this plumbing business to survive even though it may remain a marginal firm. We must note that although this firm did not do much in terms of marketing, the fact that it has a known characteristic of being ethical is almost a substitute for good advertising. This, again, indicates that good marketing and good ethics do overlap significantly.

The lower-right quadrant of Exhibit 6-1 is the worst scenario. Once again, without being concerned about the causal relationships, a company that has a dangerous product and does much aggressive and misleading advertising is likely to find itself in a disastrous situation. The Dalkon Shield was one such product. This particular birth control device (IUD, intrauterine device) caused so many cancer cases, and so many of these cases were settled in and out of courts for very large sums, that the company finally went bankrupt.

By reconsidering Exhibit 6-1, two conditions come to focus that need to be elaborated further. These are (1) good marketing with poor ethics could be and often is profitable, and (2) good ethics with poor marketing is also a viable proposition. Robin and Reidenbach propose that marketing strategy must be connected to ethics in that "corporations should be concerned about something more than making money" (1987, 45). They maintain further that good ethics and good marketing may not only coexist but may create excellence. They refer to Peters and Waterman's book, *In Search of Excellence*, for support of their stance (1982). However, when Robin and Reidenbach discuss in passing the Nestle's baby formula example, they are implicitly supporting the fact that good marketing programs without good ethics still could yield profits. Nestle developed and marketed the baby formula in many third-world countries, despite objections and ethical questions. Thousands of babies died because of poor handling of the product, yet the company continued to make money. Of course, it could have made more money by avoiding the subsequent controversy and boycotts to its products. However, with the exception of outside public pressures, there were no business or economic forces that would necessitate the company's combining good marketing with good ethics. A more dramatic example is provided by Babcock and Wilcox, the manufacturers of nuclear power plants. Even though there are no solutions to nuclear waste, and the accumulated nuclear waste is a serious threat to the globe, the company continues to produce nuclear power plants. Here is an example of good marketing with questionable ethics. But Babcock and Wilcox opt to survive and make money first. If there are no controls over their behavior, they will continue in the same manner they always have.

Perhaps the second condition is even more critical. If good ethics prevail, without good marketing the firm still could survive. General Dynamics has used poor marketing practices by overcharging the U.S. government on military contracts. However, it has invested heavily in a program to increase future ethical behavior in the company. The program includes not only a series of seminars to communicate the importance of ethical behavior to its employees, but also a "squeal clause." This squeal clause protects those who bring unethical behavior to the attention of the proper individuals. Furthermore, it rewards them (Markowitz and Byrne 1985). Under these circumstances, if General Dynamics successfully implements the ethics program despite its questionable marketing practices in the past, it can survive. However, good ethics with poor marketing is more applicable to small local businesses. Some small communities protect small local firms that behave ethically, even if they do not use effective marketing. People of the community knowingly support these businesses even though they may not be up to date, they may not carry modern products, they may not have good salespeople, and even if they have poor location, poor pricing, and poor merchandising.

WHAT ARE THE PROBLEMS PREVENTING THE COEXISTENCE OF GOOD MARKETING AND GOOD ETHICS?

The fact that poor ethics can coexist with good marketing and the company can survive and still make money is perhaps the most problematic area in the four scenarios presented in Exhibit 6-1. The market conditions, competition, or legal structure do not have enough pressure on the firm to take an ethical stance.

Discrepancy between the law and ethics creates significant room for what may be considered unethical behavior. Although R. J. Reynolds has been under attack not to market Uptown™, a new brand of cigarettes specifically targeted at African Americans, legally the company is free to do so. Many people complained about the fact that the advertisements were designed to take advantage of a vulnerable group and, hence, they were not ethical.

Certain nonprofit health advocacy groups maintained that although African Americans drink less than whites on average, nonetheless they suffer twice as much cirrhosis and other liver diseases. Also, the rate of cancer in African American males ages 35 to 44 is 10 times that of whites. Despite these facts, alcohol and tobacco producers have embarked on aggressive marketing programs to promote their products in this market segment (Young 1990). Legally, these companies are completely free to act as they wish. From an ethical perspective, their behavior easily can be questioned.

Once again, if perfect competition was to prevail in the marketplace, there would be little or no deviations from good marketing and a good ethics position. Those firms that would deviate from this position would lose their market position and cease to survive. Under today's market conditions, which are far removed from Adam Smith's perfectly competitive market, a firm (in fact, perhaps, most firms) deviates from the ideal situation of good ethics and good marketing. When pressures do not exist for the desired ethical behavior, then it is up to the individual entrepreneur or the particular company (whichever the case may be) to behave ethically. This becomes an optional matter and may be decided based on the degree of motivation the decision makers may have to behave ethically.

Exhibit 6-2 illustrates different pressures a decision maker is likely to experience in regard to certain ethical decisions. First and foremost, every person has a cognitive moral development stage that will screen the ethical problem and interpret it (Ferrell, Gresham, and Fraedrich 1989; Ferrell and Fraedrich 1991). Thus, each decision maker may perceive an ethical issue differently based on his or her background and sensitivity toward these issues. But there are two other groups of mediating variables, and these may play an

Exhibit 6-2
Ethical Motivation of the Decision Maker

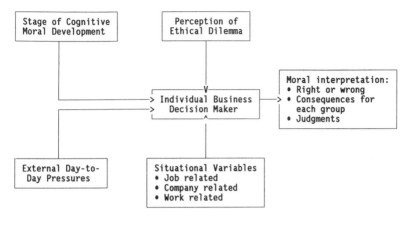

even more critical role in ethics-related decisions. These two groups of mediating variables are external day-to-day pressures and situational variables (see Exhibit 6-2).

External Day-to-Day Pressures

Day-to-day pressures are extremely critical because they are related to the immediate survival instincts of the individual decision maker. It is maintained here (perhaps unfortunately) that the survival instinct is more basic than instincts to do good to others or ethical behavior. Perhaps a simpler example of this is the Donner Pass episode, which is a black page in American history. Civilized people were trapped on a snow-covered mountain and they resorted to cannibalism and ate each other. Thus, when a marketing decision maker is in a situation with survival at stake, it is quite reasonable to assume that the survival instinct will overcome the instinct to behave ethically. If an entrepreneur is at the borderline of bankruptcy, he or she may not take ethical behavior as seriously as survival, and hence may resort to unethical means to survive. Thus, the survival instinct is a very powerful mediator and more fundamental than other considerations.

Situational Variables

Situational variables relate to factors in the environment (Trevino 1986). However, these variables are separated from day-to-day survival factors. There are basically three groups of factors: job related, company related, and work related (see Exhibit 6-2). Job-related factors deal with factors influencing promotion advancements and other specific job-related variables. Company-related factors associate to specific features of the company that will influence the individual decision maker such as the corporate culture, supervisors, union relationships, and so on. Work-related factors deal specifically with the work to be performed. Specific factors include the role to be played, the risk to be taken, the process to be used, and so on.

When the decision maker perceives an ethical dilemma, this perception is mediated significantly by these factors. The decision maker at this point makes a moral interpretation based on what is right and what is wrong on the basis of personal thinking. Ferrell, Gresham, and Fraedrich (1989) termed this factor *deontological*. Furthermore, the decision maker evaluates consequences of the decision on each and every group involved in the ethical dilemma under consideration. Ferrell, Gresham, and Fraedrich termed this factor *teleological*. Finally, at the judgmental phase, the individual judges the alternatives to decide which alternative is most ethical and which is most desirable. Unfortunately, at this point good marketing decisions may part company with good ethics. At least four specific conditions in modern-day marketing are influencing ethical decisions in the direction of rather poor ethics: (1) lack of ethical values or orientation, (2) survival instincts, (3) situational factors, and (4) short-term orientation.

1. Most decision makers, or for that matter, most people in our society do not have a background that leads to certain ethical values. This background may or may not be church or religion related. It simply stems from enlightened self-interest, which implies that one's overall well-being is related closely to the well-being of those who are around that person. Thus, one's well-being can be enhanced primarily if and when the well-beings of all of the significant others around that person are enhanced. However, in this day and age of the "me" generation, which demands immediate gratification, this kind of orientation does not exist in large measure.

2. The power of survival instincts already has been discussed in

this chapter. Particularly in situations in which the decision maker perceives the situation as one of survival, ethical considerations take a secondary position vis-à-vis the survival considerations, especially in recession times when many firms are at the brink of failure. This kind of orientation can become serious and at times even a menace to consumers. Retailers at the brink of failure that try to sell consumers foodstuffs after their specified dates or selling defective and faulty products are not uncommon, particularly in many low-income and other inner-city areas.

3. Situations influencing an ethical stance or ethics-related decisions are so numerous and at times so complex that some authors refer to this factor-decision-related area as *situational ethics*. Here, the consideration of every case separately without a general stance and the making of inconsistent decisions do nothing but cause hardship for consumers. However, situational ethics is almost a part of today's business life.

As this book is written, downsizing in the corporate world is almost an epidemic. It is quite possible that many people will do anything to keep their jobs, including behaving unethically and causing problems for consumers.

4. Short-term orientation has become very problematic for the American society as a whole as well as for the business sector. When short-term results become dominant in the decision-making process, many business decision makers are likely to make decisions that will make them or their company look good. This kind of orientation is likely to influence their moral interpretations (see Exhibit 6-2). The outcome of these moral interpretations is likely to be anticonsumer, antiunion, and so on. No doubt many of the savings and loan (S&L) decisions leading to the S&L crises in the late 1980s and early 1990s in the United States were based on this type of short-term orientation. As with survival instincts, this orientation has the power of causing decisions that are questionable ethically.

POCKETBOOK ETHICS

Most of the decisions relating to the four factors discussed in the preceding section are related to the individual's or the company's income or economic well-being. Unfortunately, in the present American market, economic well-being has become such an important force that most ethically related decisions are influenced by this force, a situation termed *pocketbook ethics*. Many business- and marketing-related decisions are made in consideration of the pocketbook. Thus, the ethical stance taken in these decisions takes its direction from pocketbook ethics. In other words, economics determines the ethical position that decision makers and companies are likely to take. This orientation on the part of decision makers could be termed anything from "ruthless" to "devastating," depending on the seriousness of the decision and its far-reaching implications in the marketplace.

SUMMARY

Although good ethics would reinforce good marketing, because of the lack of competition and the lack of conditions that Adam Smith envisioned, good ethics are not necessarily practiced in today's marketing. It is discussed in this chapter that good marketing (perhaps it may be referred to as shrewd marketing) without good ethics still can be quite profitable. Although the decision makers could take an ethical stance in all of their decisions, conditions in their day-to-day activities are such that they may not take such a stance. Because much of the time the decision makers lack ethical values and background, they are driven by their survival instincts, they face many situational variables, and they are oriented to short-term success, good ethics and good marketing do not coexist regularly.

Thus, in today's marketing, just a basic ethical orientation is not a necessity and often is not practiced regularly. Hence, it is reasonable to say (unfortunately) that ethics in today's markets do not work automatically. This is because those who are in power to make ethical decisions are sidetracked by many other forces.

REFERENCES

Cullen, John B., Bart Victor, and Carroll Stephens. 1989. "An Ethical Weather Report: Assessing the Organization's Ethical Climate." *Organizational Dynamics* (Autumn):50–62.

"Do Good Ethics Ensure Good Profits?" 1989. *Business and Society Review* (Summer):4–10.

Ferrell, O. C., Larry Gresham, and John Fraedrich. 1989. "A Synthesis of

Ethical Decision Models for Marketing." *Journal of Macromarketing* (Fall):55–64.

Ferrell, O. C., and John Fraedrich. 1991. *Business Ethics*. Boston: Houghton Mifflin Company.

Markowitz, Daniel B., and John A. Byrne. 1985. "Where Business Goes to Stock Up on Ethics." *Business Week* (October 14):63, 66.

Peters, Tom, and Robert H. Waterman, Jr. 1982. *In Search of Excellence*. New York: Alfred A. Knopf.

Robin, Donald P., and Eric Reidenbach. 1987. "Social Responsibility, Ethics and Marketing Strategy: Closing the Gap between Concept and Application." *Journal of Marketing* (January):44–58.

Smith, Adam. 1779. *Wealth of Nations*. London: George Routledge.

Trevino, Linda K. 1986. "Ethical Decision Making in Organizations: A Person-Situation Interactionist Model." *Academy of Management Review* (July):601–618.

Young, Lawrence E. 1990. "Ads Targeting Blacks Become Blacks' Target." *Dallas Morning News*, May 20, sec. B p. 12.

7 | Social Responsibility from a Consumerism Perspective

Thus far we have seen that social responsibility is necessary because competition is not keen enough to enforce ethical behavior on the part of the business sector. Furthermore, consumers do not have equal opportunity and there are a number of pathological circumstances in marketing.

Being a consumer in a complex society has many advantages. Among these are the variety of product and brand choices consumers have, the information to which they have access, some degree of protection against dangerous products, and legal options if they so desire. Of course, there are many more.

However, many of these advantages also can pose problems that would baffle, if not totally discourage, the consumer. Furthermore, many marketing situations in the complex society can be physically or at least economically damaging, if not totally dangerous. In a typical supermarket, there are now more than 10,000 products. Most of these (approximately 90%) did not even exist 10 years ago. Over 20,000 people are estimated to be harmed by defective products (Product Safety Commission Annual Report). There are more than 40,000 products in a department store from which to choose. An average consumer receives some 1500 commercial messages daily. Many of these messages make conflicting statements that decrease the likelihood of consumers' making rational (or at least reasonable) decisions.

What are some of the conditions that would baffle the consumer?

The circumstances that contribute to consumer dissatisfaction are discussed in this chapter under two categories: (1) under normal conditions, and (2) when the conditions deviate from normalcy. After having explored these two major sets of circumstances and consumerism's response to them, an attempt is made to propose the ideal circumstances for consumers in a complex society.

CONSUMER DISSATISFACTION UNDER NORMAL CONDITIONS

Assuming no foul play intended on the part of the manufacturer or the marketer, there are some conditions stemming from the complexity of the society that baffle the consumer. Three such key factors are considered in this section: (1) choice, (2) lack of information, and (3) lack of ability to cope.

Consumer Choice

The choices that American consumers face are overwhelming. Considering the fact that in their daily lives they consume or use less than about 1000 to 2000 products, the offering of 10,000 brands in the supermarket or some 40,000 brands in a major department store may be viewed as baffling. Since consumers typically are restricted by time and budgetary constraints in their purchase decisions, and since brand information does not come in a standard format (i.e., products are not offered with standardized information packages or marketing techniques), the choice decision may be seen as difficult. Whether or not the individual should buy an Apple, IBM, Zenith, or another personal computer (PC) is not an easy decision. In many cases when the information is available, the consumer cannot possibly compare hundreds of products and optimize a purchase decision.

Lack of Information

For a consumer who has an inquiring mind and likes to ask questions and make comparisons, it sometimes is difficult to make a decision on some of the simplest purchases. Should he or she buy a slightly more expensive dishwasher detergent "that enables you to see yourself in the china," or one that has a lower price, or one at the same price but with certain additives? Should he or she buy an imported economy car, domestic economy car, foreign economy car produced domestically, medium-sized car with more comfort, a large gas guzzler for absolute luxury, or what? Should the consumer buy into a diet plan, join a health spa, or have a personal trainer? All of these have many subdecision areas and one hardly can be rational in making a series of specific decisions for one's daily life. It is difficult enough to make good choices when alternatives are plentiful, but the problem becomes magnified if information for these purchase choices may not be readily available. Although the information may be available, the time, effort, and, sometimes, the cost of obtaining this information can make it almost prohibitive. Thus, the modern consumer who takes being a consumer seriously may have many difficult problems to overcome.

Lack of Ability to Cope

In considering the lack of ability to cope, assume, for instance, that the typical consumer has had the psychological and physical resources to gather the required information, can she or he assimilate this information in such a way so that she or he can arrive at a logical and/or reasonable choice decision?

Several studies have indicated that the actual information acquisition is rather low as opposed to the expressed desire on the part of the consumers to acquire information (Jacoby, Chestnut, and Silberman 1977). This may indicate a lack of ability to assimilate product information. After a few tries, consumers simply may have given up because of the immensity of the task. All consumers are not endowed equally with information-processing capabilities and motivation, and hence some consumers may find it difficult to analyze the data that are gathered and to utilize them for product-related decisions.

This lack of ability to cope in the marketplace may be exacerbated by at least four different factors:

1. *Time Constraints.* The ampleness of the complex information and the presence of numerous calculations and comparisons to be performed make it difficult for the average individual to make decisions. As the number of product categories on the consumer's shop-

ping list increase, the nutritional information sought does not increase proportionately. In fact, there is a reverse tendency (i.e., not to seek out as much information) (Jacoby, Chestnut, and Silberman 1977). This situation may be due to a time constraint.

2. *Know-how Constraints.* Regardless of the intelligence level of the consumer, the average consumer usually does not have the knowledge needed to make intelligent marketplace decisions. This know-how constraint is viewed as an additional factor in decreasing consumers' ability to cope in the marketplace.

3. *Mental Constraints.* Unlike the first two constraints above, emphasis here is on the consumer with less-than-average mental capacity. The ability to cope in the marketplace for these consumers diminishes in large proportions. These people may have difficulty in making reasonable decisions under rather nontrying conditions, but when the complexity is such that the conditions become too trying, their frailties may become even more evident. Chapter 5 presents a more detailed discussion of consumer frailties.

4. *Chronological Constraints.* The increasing numbers of the elderly and their purchasing power make this segment an extremely important one (Linden 1986; Lumpkin 1985). However, consumers in this segment, particularly those over 65 or 70 years of age, have certain needs that are unmet. Furthermore, they become very dependent on certain services, such as those of a pharmacist. They need better advice and better products in health-related areas and in financial matters. As they become more and more dependent on these products and services, they become more and more vulnerable as consumers.

As can be seen from our discussion, the complexity of the society and the degree of bafflement on the part of the consumer may be somewhat proportionate to each other. The increasing complexity is viewed as a major factor in creating a certain degree of confusion and difficulty for the consumer. In addition to these problems that come about by inadvertent and indirect institutional-societal means of growth and change, there are additional and more direct problems. These are the problems that are created more directly by the marketing institution itself. The following section of this chapter deals with certain manipulative actions practiced by marketing organizations that add to consumer problems and enhance their complexity many times over.

CONSUMER DISSATISFACTION WHEN THE CONDITIONS DEVIATE FROM NORMALCY

In addition to the natural complexities based on the growth and change in our society that create direct and indirect hardships on consumers, there are hardships created through questionable marketing practices. There are at least three groups of questionable marketing practices: pricing, advertising, and product design.

Questionable Practices in Pricing: Discrimination and the Consumer

In Chapter 4, we discuss the myth of the equal opportunity consumer. Marketing practices related to pricing include those that create direct or indirect discrimination. There are many different discriminatory practices in marketing. Many of these practices are concentrated particularly in the pricing area. Discrimination in marketing leads directly or indirectly to some consumers' not having equal opportunity to buy certain goods and services. Numerous questionable pricing practices are particularly discriminatory. In this section, three types of discrimination are identified: (1) overt discrimination, (2) covert discrimination, and (3) de facto discrimination.

Overt Discrimination

In many facets of our business sector, intentionally or unintentionally, different individuals are charged different prices. Although there may be some good excuses on the part of the businesspeople as to why different prices might be charged for different people, there hardly is sufficient moral justification. The following episode illustrates this point.

A Mexican American couple and an African American couple shopped a number of appliance stores. Despite their very similar credit profiles, the African American couple was charged 49% interest for an 18-month period, whereas the Mexican American couple was charged 82% interest for 18 months (Sturdivant 1968).

Overt discrimination is not necessarily racial; it also may be economic. Many professionals such as doctors, dentists, and attorneys manage to charge what the market can bear or what the clients can afford. Similarly, in many parts of the country where there are large numbers of people who may be considered poor, there are multiple prices (Caplovitz 1963). This situation may prevail to the point that *the customer has to ask "how much?"* (Caplovitz 1963). The response to such a question is rather arbitrary and depends upon to what extent the merchant may consider the customer a "good" or "bad" risk. It has been customary to hear about the prices going up when certain people in the inner city receive their welfare checks. In dentists' or doctors' offices, the first bits of information that are required is if the individual is employed, what the occupation is, and if there is insurance to cover costs partially or fully. All of these questions lead to discriminatory charges based on the individual's ability to pay, rather than the nature of the service delivered.

Covert Discrimination

The consumer price index (CPI) presumably indicates the changes in overall prices for the "average American." However, there is no reason to assume that the changing cost of living is the same for all income groups. Different income groups have different consumption patterns reflected in their "market baskets." Furthermore, price increases or decreases are different for the product categories included in these market baskets. For example, price increases for new cars, for used cars, and for public transportation are not equal. If the staple food prices go up faster than fancy food prices, and if one group spends more on staple foods than other groups, that group's cost of living goes up faster than other groups. Thus, cost of living changes are not proportionate for all income groups. Two studies have indicated that, for blacks as well as for low-income consumers in general, the cost of living has gone up faster than for the rest of the society (Samli 1969, 1971). It is doubtful that these trends have been reversed. This outcome is based on such facts as whether the costs of public transportation or used cars have gone up faster than the prices of new cars. Similarly, rents have increased faster than the price of privately bought housing. This type of covert discrimination worsens the relative position of the poor and other minorities.

De Facto Discrimination

Unlike the first two types of discrimination, de facto discrimination is meant to imply that, after the fact, the consumer has been discriminated against because she or he did not have a choice when buying at a place where prices are known to be higher.

One study reports that a group of poor families, in order to take advantage of a local emergency relief program, had to fill out forms and follow instructions (Samli 1972). The local major grocery stores refused to participate in the required red tape. As a result, the poor families bought their groceries from local mom-and-pop stores, paying 5% to 10% higher prices. Marcus (1969) reported that mom-and-pop outlets charge substantially higher prices. Those who are forced to go to these stores because they do not have transportation, or those who are forced to go to these stores because of language limitations (they speak only Spanish), are forced to pay higher prices and hence experience de facto price discrimination.

One may consider the situations in which all three types of discrimination may coexist simultaneously. This is quite a likelihood. Caplovitz's theory (1963) of the "poor pay more" is still quite relevant. The conditions may have become even worse.

Questionable Practices in Advertising

Many years ago, Kendall (1971) asserted that advertising's specific role in the marketing function is to convey the news and the benefits of the product to the consumer. In this context, at least five negative functional attributes of advertising can be identified: failure to inform, manipulation, deception, targeting vulnerable consumers, and causing undesirable accumulation of economic power.

Failure to Inform

In a complex society such as ours in which production and consumption are divorced from each other many times over, if there is no proper communication, mass production and mass consumption cannot be coordinated. *Proper communication* means informative advertising. Thus the "factual" and "emotional" aspects of advertising have been the subjects of great controversy (Kendall 1971; Jones 1969; Aaker 1982b).

Although it cannot be shown decisively that advertising intentionally avoids being factual, in the process of being over involved in emotionalism it is quite possible that at times advertising ignores being factual. This situation may not serve those consumers well who are in the marketplace who need more information than the simple and emotionally laden information transmitted by marketers. Thus, by not arming the consumer with the much-needed information, advertising not only may not fulfill its basic function of informing the consumer, it may be argued that, as a societal institution, advertising may not be utilizing our national resources in the most desirable way. Since consumers are not well informed, they may not make "good" decisions in the marketplace. National priorities that dictate the utilization of societal resources may be diverted through the powerful influence of advertising as a societal institution. Failure to inform on the part of advertising can be extremely costly to all consumers.

Manipulation

Manipulation is one of the key objections to advertising. Aaker identified three different forms of possible manipulation by advertising (1982a, 193):

First, there is concern with the use of motivation research, the appeal to motives at the subconscious level. Second, there is the use of indirect emotional appeal. Finally, there is the more general claim of the power of scientific advertising to persuade—to make people believe things and behave in ways that are not in their own society's best interest.

Motivation research was rather controversial in the 1950s. This is an approach that utilizes the Freudian psychoanalytic model of consumer decision making. It assumes that stronger buying motives are recognized at the unconscious level. Consumers are not cognizant of the motives' existence and cannot articulate them consciously (Engel, Kollat, and Blackwell 1983). A consumer may dislike prunes because subconsciously she or he may associate them with old age or a domineering mother (Dichter 1960). A consumer may prefer a cake mix that requires addition of an egg because at certain stage in life it substitutes for procreation for an older woman (Dichter 1960). Similarly, a consumer may not like instant coffee because unknowingly it is associated with being uncaring or being a poor planner as a homemaker.

A book by Vance Packard, *The Hidden Persuaders* (1957), made the concept against motivation research even more controversial. As a result, it was felt that advertising could emphasize subconscious motives and influence people's choices in ways that may be called "manipulative." Although subsequent evidence dismissed the earlier accusations against motivation research by asserting that the technique is rather difficult to apply (Bachrach 1959; Engel, Kollat, and Blackwell 1983), there is still enough controversy as to advertising's manipulative capabilities.

A somewhat more advanced and definitely a more controversial form of using manipulative motivation in advertising is related to dealing with the subconscious through subliminal advertising. Although many have dismissed subliminal motivation as an unlikely story, there are others who claim that it very much exists and is very powerful.

Indirect emotional appeals imply that when advertising communicates with the consumer it utilizes approaches or associations that go beyond communicating the basic factual information. It manipulates by using emotional appeals (Bauer and Greyser 1968). In such cases, the consumer will be led to make decisions that are less than optimal (Aaker 1982a). In fact, this type of orientation can lead to deception in that it misleads and exaggerates. It furthermore does not allow the consumer to rationalize purchase behavior. Many cosmetic and shampoo commercials appear to be leaning in this direction. After all, as was stated by the president of Revlon, they all are selling "hope."

Power of advertising implies the existence of some raw power that simply manipulates consumers against their own will power (Aaker 1982b). Not only do many companies have power to use a very large number of advertising exposures to influence consumers, but they also utilize highly sophisticated scientific techniques. These techniques are claimed to modify consumer behavior patterns in the direction of a less than "rational manner."

Deception

Deception in advertising is the opposite of advertising's basic mission of providing information for consumer decision making. This situation will cause economic or other forms of injury (Aaker 1982b). Most of the deceptive advertising practices can be deduced from the Creative Code of the American Association of Advertising Agencies (1962):

1. False or misleading statements or exaggerations
2. False testimonials by competent witnesses
3. Misleading price claims

4. Disparaging competitors' products or services
5. Unsupported claims
6. Indecent statements, suggestions, or pictures

When Ford, Chrysler, and GM all claim they have the best built cars, or all of the light beer makers claim that their brand is the most popular, these may be seen as "false" statements or exaggerations. Deceptive advertising practices imply, first, that the perception of the product as relayed by an advertising message differs from reality, and, second, the same perception has a detrimental effect on the consumer's buying behavior (Aaker 1982b).

Regarding deceptive advertising, Aaker (1982b) distinguished five distinct situations. First, the entire advertisement could be deceptive; second, there could be an ambiguous statement in the ad; third, there could be a misleading silence in which more disclosure is needed as to the expected performance of the product; fourth, the ad could have a material untruth; and fifth, the ad may attempt "trade puffing," which is achieved by subjective statements of superiority or by downright exaggeration.

Targeting Vulnerable Consumers

As is discussed in various chapters of this book (see Chapters 4 and 5), some consumers are considered to be more vulnerable (or frail) than others. In recent years, heavy advertising by Reebok and Nike geared to minority teenagers has caused much social unrest and gang fights in some of the major cities. It has been claimed that the ownership of these athletic shoes has become so important that some teens would almost "kill" for them. The same types of claims have been made for tobacco and liquor advertising targeted to minorities and to women. If these groups are truly vulnerable and if advertising can cause such problems, there may be a need for more careful scrutiny.

Undesirable Accumulation of Economic Power

The undesirable accumulation of economic power is basically the aftermath of the first three negative functional attributes of advertising (i.e., failure to inform, manipulation, and deception). These three attributes and excessive advertising budgets can distort the competitive position of a firm easily. A firm could achieve an unjustified competitive advantage leading to substantial economic power based on large profits. Certainly, if questionable advertising practices continue unchecked, the accumulated economic power of firms conducting misguided (and misguiding) advertising can propagate further, leading to further abuses of the advertising institution. Currently, American firms have been very busy buying and selling each other. All of these activities are creating oligopolies and limiting competition. Along with this reduced competition, companies have more power to use certain types of advertising and accumulate additional power.

Questionable Practices in Product Design

Questionable practices in product design and marketing are very critical issues for the marketing practitioner as well as the consumer. One evidence of the seriousness of the problem is the fact that as early as 1978 manufacturers and retailers paid an estimated $2.75 billion for product liability insurance. This figure had more than doubled between 1975 and 1978 ("The Devils in the Product Liability Laws" 1979). The number of vehicles that were recalled went up from 1.5 million in 1975 to 10.7 million in 1978. Some 14.5 million auto tires were recalled during the same period ("The Devils" 1979). All of these figures skyrocketed during the following decade.

The Product Safety Commission reports some 20,000 or so injuries per year due to defective products. Many children's toys and cereals have been found dangerous or unhealthy. Faulty designs in children's car seats and cribs caused large numbers of infant mortalities.

The overall problem can be analyzed from at least five different perspectives: (1) design deficiency, (2) defective products, (3) inadequate research, (4) dangerous products, and (5) environmentally offensive products. These product-related problems, in general terms, are associated with marketing pathology, discussed in Chapter 2. More marketing-related specifics are discussed next so that these practices can be better understood and perhaps remedied.

1. Design deficiency could be critical in terms of the product's not functioning well or its being dangerous. Because of design deficiency, the product may waste excessive amounts of fuel or may not function efficiently. These situations are costly to the individual as well as to society. The manufacturer that is not keeping up with technological advances easily may be contributing to the design

deficiency problem ("The Devils" 1979; Trombeta 1980). A collision case, for instance, illustrates an example of deficient product design. It involved a defective gearshift knob. Upon collision, the gearshift knob shattered and pierced a passenger's spine, causing permanent paralysis below the point of injury (Trombeta 1980). Similar situations led to the demise of the Ford Pinto. Its gas tank was so close to the back fender of the car that it caught fire immediately upon sudden collision.

2. Defective products exist even though product design is not deficient. Defective products could be more dangerous than deficient designs because the defects are not expected. Typically, the useful safe life of the product is the time during which the product reasonably can be expected to perform in a safe manner. Defective products are likely to fall short of this definition and hence cause frustration, financial loss, or some degree of danger for the owner.

3. Inadequate product research has complicated consumers' lives further. From thalidomide to cyclamates or from Red Dye No. 2 to Rely, many products have appeared in the market that sooner or later proved to be dangerous to the consumers' well-being. This situation is caused primarily by the lack of adequate research and development (R&D) and consumer research on the part of the manufacturers. Similar claims can be made for products that may not be dangerous to the well-being of the consumers directly but may not function well or may not satisfy consumer needs adequately ("The Devils" 1979; Trombeta 1980; Nader 1968).

4. Dangerous products are the extreme negative consequences of products analyzed from any one of the three problem product perspectives above (i.e., poor design, product defects, and/or inadequate research). Some products are dangerous enough to be deadly. Others may have a long-range devastating impact not only for the individual but also for the society. The latter impact is particularly important in genetic terms. For example, heavy radiation or certain chemicals create a direct genetic impact in terms of offspring abnormalities (Bishop and Hubbard 1969). Certain architectural flaws have made certain atomic reactors particularly dangerous. They caused the Chernobyl incident in Russia, which caused cancer for thousands of Russians.

5. Environmentally dangerous products are those that may influence our soil, water, or air and make the globe less habitable in the

long run. Use of certain pesticides and insecticides has polluted the soil and the water. Sulfur and other chemicals coming from smokestacks of factories are causing major problems in the air. Emissions from auto exhausts are causing even more important problems. There are many products causing environmental damage and therefore perhaps endangering the future of the world.

CONSUMERISM AS A RESPONSE

Consumerism as a formal movement in the American market coincides with the emergence of the marketing concept. Its momentum implies some degree of failure on the part of the marketing concept. It may be maintained that it was triggered directly by Ralph Nader's auto safety investigation (Nader 1957). However, the four rights that were set forth by President Kennedy had set the foundation and the general direction of the consumerism movement in the United States (Kennedy 1963). These rights are discussed briefly in Chapter 5.

Despite the systematic manifestation of these rights and supportive legislation, the baffled status of the consumer, coupled with the conditions deviating from normalcy as discussed at the beginning of this chapter, are keeping heavy pressure on marketing thinking and practice. American consumers still expect better product performance and reliability. As these expectations are heightened, products are improved. However, with these improvements, product complexity also increases (McQuade 1972). Even though the original product may have become more reliable, because of the heightened complexity there are new and greater possibilities for malfunction and even for changes (Durden 1970).

American consumers still expect proper information so that they perhaps can have a chance to make reasonable purchase decisions. Yet there is evidence to indicate that the typical budget is not able to make decisions leading to best buys (Friedman 1966).

American consumers still expect advertisements to be factual, informative, and particularly useful in discriminating valuable product information. However, a number of studies have found that about 35–40% of the public believes that advertising is critically misleading (Bauer and Greyser 1968).

In regard to marketing thought, the consumerism movement has brought about significant deepening and broadening activity in the field. Kotler and Levy (1969), Kotler and Zaltman (1971), and others maintained that marketing's parameters are much broader than those that have been accepted until recently. Because the marketing process is applicable to many nonprofit undertakings, its impact is very far-reaching. Private universities, hospitals, churches, and many other nonprofit institutions are involved in marketing so that they can broaden their constituencies and gain further legitimacy (Samli and Sirgy 1982).

The deepening of marketing has been described by Enis (1973) in terms of developing operational marketing theories and testing in real marketing situations. He argued that the gap between marketing theory and practice can and should be narrowed (Samli and Sirgy 1982). Thus, the consumerism movement, even if only nominally, has forced the marketing thinkers and practitioners to reorganize their thinking and redirect their efforts. Many consumerist groups have been vocal and have kept watchful eyes on the products and services that appear in the market.

IDEAL CIRCUMSTANCES IN A COMPLEX SOCIETY

Perhaps the most important assertion that is being made in this chapter is that marketing, consumerism, and consumer well-being should not be treated independently of one another. In fact, if marketing fulfills its mission in the society, it will, in essence, overlap significantly with the role of the consumerism movement. Furthermore, only when consumer well-being is optimized in a society will marketing as a societal institution be perceived as providing a significant and legitimate function in society. Taking this position as a "given" in this chapter, the following sections attempt to raise some critical issues as to the specific goals of marketing.

Elimination of the Baffled Consumer

Assuming that marketing and the consumer's well-being are two sides of the same equation, then marketing's role is perceived to be the enhancement of consumer well-being. That is, consumer well-being is a function of the marketing institution. This implies eliminating the baffled status of the consumers.

It must be understood that eliminating the baffled status does not mean that the society must regress and go back to less complex forms of society. Rather, it means resolving consumer problems with progressive and effective marketing. This can be done through proactive marketing. Proactive marketing may resolve consumer problems as it strives for greater rewards in an open market system in terms of greater profits. Proactive marketing here implies the positive leadership that the discipline provides for the society in resolving consumer problems. Thus, the second most important assertion in this chapter is that marketing in society must function in a proactive manner, providing leadership in terms of solving (and helping prevent) consumer problems.

Mutual Responsibilities Leading to Mutual Benefit

If the premise that the general well-being of the consumers in the society is in the best interest of marketing, and marketing can deliver such an end, then the question must be raised as to how such an end can be achieved. This situation can be explained with a simple example. The reader should note that this is only an example. Some 20% of the American populace is considered to be below the poverty threshold. If somehow they were to be brought into the mainstream of American market economy, the profit-rewards of marketing would be increased by at least 20%. If marketing can bring these individuals into the mainstream by stimulating the economy and by aiding them to purchase goods and services, there hardly could be any other type of aftermath but economic progress.

As discussed in this chapter, marketing practices are oftentimes questionable. Somehow, the desired goal in the society is mutual satisfaction between marketing and society. However, since this is not an automatic given, it is necessary for the society to attempt to reach the desired goal by resorting to consumer education, consumer information, and consumer protection. These were discussed in Chapter 5.

SUMMARY

This chapter delves into the issues of the all-important social responsibility of marketing from a consumerism perspective. The discussion first revolves around the baffled status of the consumer. This particular status is caused by the abundance of choice, lack of information, and lack of ability on the part of the consumer to assimilate existing information.

The conditions become more serious for the consumer as consumer discrimination and questionable marketing practices are brought into an already complicated picture. Three types of discrimination are identified: overt, covert, and de facto discrimination. Also, questionable marketing practices can be detected in the areas of advertising and product design.

It is maintained in this chapter that the consumerism movement still is going strong. This strength, at least partially, is due to the failure of the marketing concept to perform the way it should. From an ideal perspective, it is in marketing's best interest to deliver consumer satisfaction and higher quality of life. For such a goal to become reality, there must be adequate consumer information, education, and protection. Without these three remedies, marketing, as a societal institution, cannot be perceived as playing a significant and legitimate role in enhancing the society and its quality of life.

REFERENCES

Aaker, David A. 1982a. "Deceptive Advertising." In *Consumerism*, edited by David A. Aaker and George S. Day, 230–248. New York: The Free Press.

Aaker, David A. 1982b. "The Social and Economic Effects of Advertising." In *Consumerism*, edited by David A. Aaker and George S. Day, 190–209. New York: The Free Press.

Aaker, David A., and George S. Day. 1982. "A Guide to Consumerism." In *Consumerism*, edited by David A. Aaker and George S. Day. New York: The Free Press.

American Association of Advertising Agencies. 1962. *Creative Code*. New York: American Association of Advertising Agencies.

Bachrach, J. J. 1959. "The Ethics of Tachistoscopy." *Bulletin of the Atomic Scientists* 15:212–215.

Bauer, Raymond A., and Stephen A. Greyser. 1968. *Advertising in America: The Consumer View*. Cambridge: Harvard University Press.

Bishop, James W., and Henry W. Hubbard. 1969. *Let The Seller Beware*. Washington, DC: National Press Inc.

Caplovitz, David. 1963. *The Poor Pay More*. New York: The Free Press.

"The Devils in the Product Liability Laws." 1979. *Business Week* (February 12):72–79.

Dichter, Ernest. 1960. *The Strategy of Desire.* Garden City, NJ: Doubleday.

Durden, M. 1970. "Consumerism and Product Quality." *Quality Progress* (July):53–59.

Engel, James F., David T. Kollat, and Robert D. Blackwell. 1983. *Consumer Behavior,* 4th ed. New York: Holt, Rinehart and Winston.

Enis, Ben. 1973. "Deepening of the Marketing Concept." *Journal of Marketing* 37 (October):35–39.

Friedman, M. Peter. 1966. "Consumer Confusion in the Selection of Supermarket Products." *Journal of Applied Psychology* (November).

Jacoby, Jacob, Robert W. Chestnut, and William Silberman. 1977. "Consumer Use and Comprehension of Nutrition Information." *Journal of Consumer Research.* (September):119–128.

Jones, Mary Gardiner. 1969. "The Cultural and Social Impact of Advertising on American Society." In *Consumerism,* 4th ed., edited by David A. Aaker and George S. Day, 210–214. New York: Free Press.

Kendall, David M. 1971. "Statement Before the Federal Trade Commission." *Federal Trade Commission Hearings.* Washington, DC: U.S. Government Printing Office.

Kennedy, John F. 1963. "Consumer Advisory Council: First Report." Executive Office of the President. Washington, DC: United States Government Printing Office, October.

Kotler, Philip, and Sidney Levy. 1969. "Broadening the Concept of Marketing." *Journal of Marketing* 33 (January):55–56.

Kotler, Philip, and Gerald Zaltman. 1971. "Social Marketing: An Approach to Planned Social Change." *Journal of Marketing* 37 (July): 3–12.

Linden, F. 1986. "The $800 Billion Market." *American Demographics* (February):4–6.

Lumpkin, J. R. 1985. "Shopping Orientation Segmentation of the Elderly Consumer." *Journal of the Academy of Marketing Science* (Spring):271–289.

McGuire, G. Patrick. 1973. *The Consumer Affairs Department Organization and Functions.* New York: Conference Board.

McQuade, Walter. 1972. "Why Nobody's Happy About Appliances." *Fortune* (May):182–190.

Marcus, Burton H. 1969. "Similarity of Ghetto and Nonghetto Food Costs." *Journal of Marketing Research* (August):365–368.

Nader, Ralph. 1957. *Unsafe at any Speed.* New York: Pocket Books.

Nader, Ralph. 1968. "The Great American Gyp." *The New York Review* (November 12).

Packard, Vance. 1957. *The Hidden Persuaders.* New York: Pocket Books.

Product Safety Commission Annual Report. (various years). Washington, DC: Product Safety Commission.

Samli, A. Coskun. 1969. "Differential Prices for the Rich and Poor." *University of Washington Business Review* (Summer):111–113.

Samli, A. Coskun. 1971. "Differential Price Indexes for the Negroes and Whites." *Mississippi Valley Business and Economic Review* (January):63–73.

Samli, A. Coskun. 1971. "De Facto Price Discrimination in the Food Purchases of Rural Poor." *Journal of Retailing* (Fall):65–73.

Samli, A. Coskun, and M. Joseph Sirgy. 1982. "Social Responsibility in Marketing." In *Marketing Theory: A Philosophy of Science Perspective*, edited by R. P. Bush and S. D. Hunt, 250–254. Chicago: American Marketing Association.

Sturdivant, Frederick D. 1968. "Better Deal for Ghetto Shoppers." *Harvard Business Review* (March–April):130–139.

Trombeta, William L. 1980. "A Marketing Manager's Primer on Product Liability." In *Public Policy Issues in Marketing*, edited by C. J. Frey, et al., 98–113. Ann Arbor, MI: University of Michigan.

8 | Developing Consumer-Friendly Products

It has been discussed thus far that consumers, in general, do not have equal opportunity initially. But when this situation is combined with worsening conditions in the market as well as with the frailty of certain consumer groups, then the need for socially proactive marketing becomes very clear. An important part of this necessary proactivity is to develop consumer-friendly products. The consumer-friendliness concept has many dimensions. But, in general terms, if a product (or products) provides the maximum amount of short-run and long-run benefits for the user without hurting other consumers, it may be considered *consumer friendly*. This chapter explores specific dimensions of consumer-friendly product development. It is maintained here that all products are not consumer friendly. Even though the product may be accepted well and be very popular in the marketplace, it should not be considered consumer friendly unless it provides adequate consumer information, it was designed with consumer protection in mind, and its features are such that the product provides a maximum amount of short-run and long-run benefits for the user without hurting other consumers who will not buy or use this product. In order to develop consumer-friendly products, it is necessary to recognize the key components of such products.

KEY COMPONENTS OF
CONSUMER-FRIENDLY PRODUCTS

Exhibit 8-1 indicates that there are three major components of consumer-friendly products: product design, consumer protection, and product information.

Product Design

All product designs are not necessarily consumer friendly. Some of the earlier models of videocassette recorders (VCRs) were so complicated one had to be very knowledgeable in order to tape multiple TV programs in advance. In fact, it was extremely difficult just to set up the clock of the VCR. Early personal computers (PCs) that claimed user friendliness often were user unfriendly. Similarly, some of the earlier models of microwaves and some of the very sophisticated models of dishwashers can be classified as consumer unfriendly. Consumer friendliness in product design rests on at least five specific criteria: simplicity, effectiveness, efficiency, integration, and storage.

    1. Simplicity. Simplicity is extremely important for effective use

Exhibit 8-1
Key Components of Consumer-Friendly Products

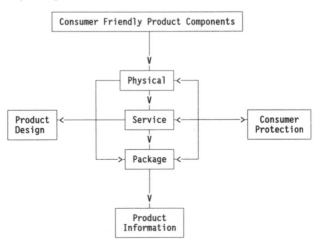

of the product. Just because a product is complex does not mean it is a good product and that it fulfills certain functions better than simpler products. Consumer-friendly products must be easy to use, easy to program, and easy to maintain.

2. *Effectiveness.* The term *effectiveness* is used to depict the congruence between the product design and consumer needs. To the extent that the product satisfies certain consumer needs well, that product is effective. In time, as the society and life-styles become more complex, the effectiveness feature is likely to become more important.

3. *Efficiency.* The product efficiency factor goes beyond consumer friendliness and enters into the area of environmental friendliness. This aspect of product design is discussed in Chapter 9. Efficiency in relationship to consumer friendliness deals with using minimum amounts of energy, fuel, and so on, for the maximum amount of work. Certainly getting 40 miles per gallon is more efficient than a gas guzzler that provides only 14 miles per gallon. Dishwashers, washers, dryers, and other appliances are all efficiency related. If purchasing and operating the product is relatively less painful, then the product is consumer friendly.

4. *Integration.* Consumers do not use just one product but multitudes of products. A consumer-friendly product is the one that fits into a system of products. This is the basic idea behind having home entertainment centers rather than just TVs, VCRs, and so on. Designing a kitchen or a bathroom for the elderly with hand rails and specially designed cabinets are also examples of integration. If a product is out of proportion, off color, out of sync in terms of its functioning with other products in the household, or it does not fit into the scheme of things in the household (or other systems like the food system or apparel system of the individual rather than the household), that product is not integrated and is less likely to be consumer friendly.

5. *Storage.* There are two specific aspects of storage. First, being able to keep the product in a specific storage area or in a designated area in the household is important. If the product is not designed to fit into certain standard storage schemes, it cannot be friendly. Second, the product's storability is related to its durability. Many consumer nondurables (e.g., groceries), semidurables (e.g., apparel), or durables (e.g., appliances) may be stored for certain periods of

time, but local and in-house atmospherics may have a significant influence on storability of products. For instance, under normal circumstances a VCR might be kept for a long time, but in more humid and dusty surroundings its life is shortened substantially. The more durable the product, the more storable it is, and therefore the more consumer friendly it becomes.

It must be reiterated that our discussion thus far has been related only to the physical aspects of product design. However, there are two other very critical aspects of a product: service and package (see Exhibit 8-1).

The more complicated or technical the product is, the greater is the need for service. In addition to installation, repair service may be needed for maintenance and for performance improvement. The easier the access to service, the more consumer friendly is the product. It also must be emphasized that quality of service in this case particularly enhances the consumer-friendliness feature of the product. The higher the quality of service, the more consumer friendly is the product.

The product package is also an important component of the product. Consumer friendliness of packaging is related to having the product properly protected, providing the consumer with necessary information about the product and its care through the packaging process, and, finally, having the package perhaps provide some value of its own. This last element could be reusable containers, reusable wrapping, or a permanent protective case, among others.

Consumer Protection

Consumers cannot possibly protect themselves from certain unknown dangers of a product. In the extreme case of thalidomide consumers could not possibly have known that this particular sleeping pill would cause abnormalities in unborn babies. However, all the cases do not have to be as extreme as this one. From the design of a mattress that is giving the individual a backache, to a headache remedy that is upsetting many users' stomachs, all are cases of consumer-unfriendly products. The degree of unfriendliness of the product is related to the degree of its negative impact. The greater the stomach upset, the greater is the consumer unfriendliness of the headache medicine.

From a consumer protection perspective, consumer safety aspects of a product need to be considered at the design stage. If the product is not designed properly, the consumer hardly can be able to protect himself or herself. It is impossible for persons to protect themselves against some negative product impact with which they are neither familiar nor expect. Furthermore, they actually have no defense for such an event. Thus, it is essential that the manufacturer has a product that is safe for consumers to use.

The safety component of the product can be evaluated by a series of questions. Exhibit 8-2 presents such a series of questions. The predicted effects of the product before it is launched are assessed on the basis of their harmfulness. Since these situations are not quite dichotomous, a five-point scale is used for the assessment process. First, two considerations, short-run and long-run, are related to side effects of the product. Typically, the mattress that causes a backache is causing side effects. Recently, silicone breast implants have been under attack for causing skin or allergic problems or even cancer. Similarly, the product in the long run may cause nervousness or allergies, and so on. Once again, the consumer protection aspect

Exhibit 8-2
A Simple Checklist for Consumer Safety

	Most Likely			Least Likely	
Are there possible short-run side effects?	1	2	3	4	5
Are there possible long-run side effects?	1	2	3	4	5
Are there possible short-run direct harmful effects?	1	2	3	4	5
Are there possible long-run direct harmful effects?	1	2	3	4	5
Is there possible short-run serious danger to life?	1	2	3	4	5
Is there possible long-run serious danger to life?	1	2	3	4	5

of product design fails. Certainly this long-run side effect is not life threatening, but it could be quite a problem for the consumer. Certain computers are claimed to cause back and eye problems in the long run that also could be major problems for the users.

Exhibit 8-2 indicates that the impact could vary from nuisance to harm and from harm to life threatening. Obviously, the differences among these three degrees of impact are not that clear-cut; however, they must be considered separately at the product development stage.

Harmful Effects

Although it may be difficult to distinguish nuisance from harmful effects, it is important to understand that many products may cause non-life-threatening harm. Many additives and chemicals that are included in prepared and frozen foods appear to be causing many different allergies. The Goldfine Group maintains that some of these allergies among children are so potent that they cause the children's classification as slow learners or uneducables. The claims are such that when these additives and chemicals are removed from the children's diet, they gain IQ points and experience major behavior modification.

A major controversy in the 1990s about dentistry surfaced and created claims and counterclaims. It was maintained by some Canadian dentists that major filling materials used by dentists are causing arthritis. Testimonials by numerous patients were used to reinforce the claims. The American Dental Association dismissed the claims despite very convincing evidence. If there is any reasonable doubt that these claims may be correct, there certainly is a potential long-term harm to the consumer.

A similar episode in late 1991 appeared in the news. Certain types of silicone used in breast implantation were claimed to be causing health disorders. They may even cause cancer. Once again, the product is not quite life threatening, but is causing a direct harmful effect.

Life-Threatening Effects

Bon Vivant soup killed many consumers because it caused botulism. This was an immediate threat to life. Asbestos, on the other hand, is accused of causing a deadly lung disease, asbestosis. This disease obviously has a life-threatening effect in the long run. Tobacco and alcohol also are accused of causing deadly diseases in the long run. In terms of more high-tech products, there have been claims that radioactivity from certain TVs and microwaves, again, may be causing cancer.

As can be seen from these few examples, products cause various degrees of threat to consumer well-being. In a proactive mode of marketing, these problems need to be solved before the product is diffused in the marketplace. Using an instrument such as the one in Exhibit 8-2, products that receive a score of 12 or less may receive a go signal. Those that receive a score of 18 or more may be put on hold, and those that receive 24 and above may be abandoned immediately.

Although there are laws providing a certain degree of consumer protection, these laws are hardly all-inclusive and cannot cover the multitude of consumer products. The laws are mainly related to (1) quantities, indicating measurements and weights of certain products; (2) qualities, dealing with safeness of certain food products; and (3) consumer safety relating to marketing products that do not comply with the safety requirements imposed by certain regulations (Keenan 1987). The laws are hardly comprehensive enough to protect the consumer from unknown or unforeseen danger.

Of course, part of the problem is related to timing. In some cases, the unforeseen or unknown problem will not surface until after many years of product use. In such cases, a company may not be able to exercise proactivity, but it could be very reactive.

Reactivity for Consumer Protection

Literature indicates that there is certain consumer complaint behavior (Day and Landon 1977; Singh 1988; Gilly 1987). This behavior is classified into three broad categories: (1) redress seeking to remedy the situation directly or indirectly by going to the seller; (2) complaining to communicate dissatisfaction for reasons other than seeking remedy; and (3) personal boycott to discontinue purchase of the offending product.

Although the marketer (or manufacturer) can simply monitor these actions and react accordingly, there is another alternative that the marketer must take. In the case of life-threatening situations or in the presence of a major harm to the consumer, the marketer simply does not have enough time just to wait for consumers to complain and then react accordingly. This type of reactive behavior would enable the firm to detect some early indicators of serious problems. The company, by being quick in its reactivity, may be able to avoid very serious problems.

Information Needs

The third component of consumer-friendly products is product information for the consumer, which some authors call consumer information. The two terms are used interchangeably.

Information Types

Exhibit 8-3 indicates that there are nine specific consumer information bits about the product: (1) economic information, (2) use information, (3) care information, (4) protective information, (5) maker identification, (6) country of origin, (7) replacement information, (8) parts information, and (9) guarantee or warranty information.

Economic information is price and value related. It may include price, price comparison, net savings, total value, unit price (price per ounce or price per pound), and so on.

Use information relates to how the product must be used so that it will yield the best results in terms of performance or in terms of energy consumption, and the like.

Care information deals with product maintenance. By knowing how to take care of the product, its long life and better service almost are assured.

Protective information primarily is related to certain warnings about the product's use. If it is not used in the specified manner, it could be dangerous; it might cause use problems, health problems, or other types of problems.

Maker identification is the brand name or manufacturer's logo, or the like. It plays an important role in reinforcing the existing corporate and brand images. Creating the product or brand image maker identification can stimulate product loyalty on the part of the consumer.

Country of origin is particularly important in international mar-

Exhibit 8-3
Information Needs for Consumer-Friendly Products

Information Bits

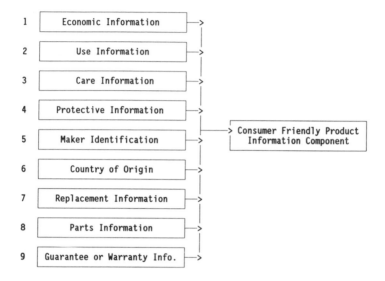

keting. By identifying from where the product is coming, the marketer is hoping to accomplish certain quality perceptions that will enable the country to sell more of its products in the world markets.

Replacement information is more typical for products that need to be replenished. If the product needs to be purchased again or certain components need to be refilled or renewed, this information is critical for the consumer to use the product properly.

Parts information is related somewhat to replacement information. If the parts of the product do not work or need to be replaced in the future, information as to how and where they could be acquired is critical for satisfactory use of the product.

Finally, many products provide information relating to warranties or guarantees that will enhance the consumer confidence in the product. Furthermore, by promising replacement or refund, the firm also will make the product more acceptable by reducing the risk regarding the product's unknown features.

Information Disseminators

The vehicle through which the product information is disseminated is a critical factor. There are a number of vehicles that will carry product-related information. The success in providing product information can be attributed at least partially to these information media. Among these are the package, the container, additional information in the container, and different forms of labels.

The package is the first disseminator of information. In time, its value as a source of information diminished as its protective and promotional features enhanced.

The container is the secondary package in which the product is placed. It provides important information about the contents of the product. It also may include price information and unit prices.

Inside the container, there may be additional information in the form of a brochure or printed and folded sheets. In more complicated products such as medicines, these sheets provide detailed technical information. Each contains facts about the contents, the use, the side effects, and so on, of a particular medicine.

Labels are different ways of posting information that is required by law about a specific product. For instance, in October 1990, the Nutrition Labeling and Education Act was enacted. It requires marketers of food products to post information regarding the amount of calories, fat, salt, and other nutrients (Brown, Kelley, and Lee 1991). Furthermore, according to this law, the Food and Drug Administration (FDA) is to regulate health messages and disease prevention claims. There are other types of labeling also. Among these are quality and performance labeling, warning labels, and care labels (Brown, Kelley, and Lee 1991).

SUMMARY

Developing a consumer-friendly product is a major social responsibility of marketing. A proactive orientation toward developing consumer-friendly products includes considerations about product design and about the physical characteristics of the product in addition to analyzing consumer protection and product information aspects of the product.

Once the physical, service, and packaging characteristics of the product are taken care of, consumer protection must be considered. In this context, the product's undesirable side effects, undesirable effects, or life-threatening effects must be considered carefully and evaluated critically before the product is launched in the marketplace.

Finally, information is critical so that the product can be purchased with confidence and used effectively. There are at least nine product information bits that must be considered and properly disseminated so that a socially responsible product can be diffused.

REFERENCES

Brown, Vernon, Craig A. Kelley, and Ming-Tung Lee. 1991. "State-of-the-Art in Labeling Research Revisited: Developments in Labeling Research 1978–1990." In *Enhancing Knowledge Development in Marketing*, edited by Mary C. Gilly et al., 717–725. Chicago: American Marketing Association.

Day, Ralph, and E. Laird Landon, Jr. 1977. "Towards a Theory of Consumer Complaining Behavior." In *Consumer and Industrial Buying Behavior*, edited by Arch Woodside, Jagdish Sheth, and Peter Bennett. Amsterdam: North-Holland Publishing Co.

Gilly, Mary C. 1987. "Post Complaint Process: From Organizational Response to Repurchase Behavior." *Journal of Consumer Affairs* (Winter):293–312.

Keenan, Denis. 1987. "Legal Aspects of Consumer Protection." *Accountancy* (November):114–117.

Singh, Jagdip. 1988. "Consumer Complaint Intentions and Behavior: Definitional and Taxonomical Issues." *Journal of Marketing* (January):93–107.

9 | *Developing Consumer-Friendly Services*

Service industries are becoming very important in our society. The medical industry, insurance industry, banking, and other financial services are among these. The relative importance of these industries is increasing due to changing life-styles in the United States. Services marketing is an expanding area of teaching, research, and practice. There is a general contention that the service component in these service industries is deteriorating. They are not producing and delivering better services. In this chapter, a discussion is presented regarding developing consumer-friendly services. After having the general parameters established for such a task, a specific example in the banking field is presented, illustrating the prevailing orientation in the marketplace and the changes that are needed to develop consumer-friendly banking services.

THE MAJOR GAPS IN SERVICES

A few years ago, Zeithaml, Parasuraman, and Berry (1985) identified four distinct gaps that exist in the service industries. These gaps are related to differences between the buyers' and sellers' perceptions. The first gap reflects the difference between consumer expectations and management perceptions of consumer expectations. The second gap deals with the difference between management perceptions of what the consumers expect and their actual service quality specifications. The third gap relates to differences between service quality specifications of the management and the service actually delivered. Finally, the fourth gap is the difference between actual service delivery and what is communicated about the service to consumers. These four gaps are discussed briefly next.

Gap 1

Service firms may not quite comprehend what high quality means to consumers and what features of the service represent those quality considerations. Since the tangible quality cues for services are very few and not defined clearly, the gap between consumer expectations and what managers think may be substantially larger than for tangible goods. The situation is worsened by the fact that service firms lag behind goods firms in their use of marketing research and in other aspects of customer orientation. Furthermore, these firms put relatively less emphasis on marketing in general. They believe that the operations function is more critical. As typically is the case in banks, for instance, this operations orientation diverts focus from consumers and reduces efforts to understand their needs and expectations (Zeithaml, Berry, and Parasuraman 1988). Banks that close their offices midafternoon or a barbershop that closes at 5:00 p.m. illustrate the point.

Gap 2

Service firms often have difficulty in matching or exceeding consumers' expectations. Zeithaml, Berry, and Parasuraman (1988) maintain that this is due to resource constraints, short-term profit orientation, market conditions, and management indifference. An overall explanation is the management's lack of commitment to service quality. The management may be too busy emphasizing cost reduction or short-term profits, which are more tangible and measurable. Finally, management perceives that consumer expectations cannot be fulfilled. The more committed the management is to this idea, the greater will be the gap between consumer expectations and management's quality specifications.

Gap 3

The discrepancy between the specifications for the service and actual delivery of the service is termed *service performance gap* by Zeithaml, et al. (1985). This situation stems from the service workers' inability to perform at the level expected by the management. In many banks, for instance, the pay scale is so low that the deliverers of the service are not quite qualified for what management intends them to do. The same situation typically plagues the whole American educational system.

Gap 4

If there are discrepancies between the actual service delivery and external communications, it may affect consumer perceptions of service quality. External communications may take place in terms of exaggerated promises or no information at all. This may affect consumers' perceptions of service quality. Zeithaml, Berry, and Parasuraman (1988) suggest that horizontal communications in organizations, which are the lateral information flows both among and within departments, can cause distorted or poor communication, which ultimately affects consumers' perception. They also emphasize the "propensity of overpromise." Because of competitive pressures, many service companies feel pressured to meet or beat competition; therefore, they may display a tendency to overpromise.

A Fifth Gap

Finally, Zeithaml, Berry, and Parasuraman (1988) discuss a fifth gap. This is basically a composite of the first four gaps and it is reflected in terms of overall service quality that is measured against five key variables: (1) tangibles, (2) reliability, (3) responsiveness, (4) assurance, and (5) empathy. These are the indicators of the five gaps. An interpretation of these variables is presented next.

1. All services have some tangible aspects or tangible impact. Here, tangible aspects of the service can be used for evaluative purposes. A dentist's office displaying how the equipment is sterilized is one such tangible aspect of a service that is being marketed.

2. The reliability factor of a service is extremely critical, particu-

larly if the service is important for the individual's well-being. If, for instance, an old lady is entrusting her total savings to a stockbroker for her retirement income, that stockbroker must be reliable and/or must deliver reliable service.

3. Closely related to reliability is responsiveness. It indicates that the deliverer of the service understands the uniqueness of the consumer's particular need. In a dance studio, the instructor, for instance, must be able to distinguish the motivated and highly talented from those who are mediocre and from those who are totally untalented. The particular dance studio that can provide different programs for these groups will be able to illustrate responsiveness.

4. Assurance is shown not only by giving an impression to the service-seeking consumer. Real assurance is providing the customer with past service performance, malpractice insurance, and a money-back guarantee that really means value.

5. Finally, empathy relates to going beyond reliability and responsiveness in that the service provider must be sympathetic with the service seeker's needs and frame of mind. The service provider must identify with the service seeker and his or her particular needs.

Having set the above model relating to gaps, quality, and responsibility of the service provider, it is necessary to put this particular frame of thought into practice. Since the services sector is extremely diversified or varied, providing an example of developing consumer-friendly services must be industry specific. The example here deals with one such attempt in regard to developing banking services that are consumer friendly.

DEVELOPING CONSUMER-FRIENDLY FINANCIAL SERVICES*

Banks and other financial institutions not only are having an identity crisis in terms of their role, position, and services, but also are having difficulty in identifying their role vis-à-vis the consumer (Bennett and Higgins 1988). The result of this identity crisis has been felt in the loss of profits. Much confusion exists about what are the most important factors in banking relationships. As banks are using computers and becoming more and more "high tech," they

*This section authored by A. Coskun Samli and Cheryl J. Frohlich.

are losing touch with their consumers' needs. This depersonalization process, which results in consumer insensitivity, is costing the banking sector. Consumer sensitivity, the raison d'être for the banking sector, is needed to provide particular guidance for the industry to become both efficient and effective.

This section posits that developing consumer-friendly financial services is the key to success. Three propositions are put forth: (1) efficiency without effectiveness results in suboptimization, (2) the parameters established in the Kennedy manifesto are insufficient to develop consumer-friendly services (Kennedy 1963), and (3) seven psychological needs of the consumer must be addressed to develop consumer-friendly services.

The Efficiency/Effectiveness Dichotomy

In order for a bank to become more consumer oriented, a distinction must be made between "efficiency" and "effectiveness." *Efficiency* is related to providing services at the lowest possible cost; in other words, minimizing the cost and maximizing output. *Effectiveness*, on the other hand, deals with the ability of delivering the service to the most appropriate market segments. If a bank produces a service efficiently but nobody cares for that service, it is ineffective. In service industries, efficiency without effectiveness does not lead to optimizing consumer satisfaction or profit.

As is illustrated in Exhibit 9-1, if the bank tries to be efficient by using computers and other technological devices without consideration of consumer needs (Panel A, Exhibit 9-1), the depersonalization of the bank services will interfere with the profit picture. The consumers' desire to have more personalized services is viewed as the effectiveness factor. If effectiveness and efficiency efforts were to be combined (Panel B, Exhibit 9-1), the bank's performance is likely to be optimized. Efficiency measures must be considered and implemented only within the constraints of consumer needs, thus taking the effectiveness factor into account. Computers and other high-tech devices cannot be used until the bank is certain that they will not add to the divergence between the delivery of products and services by the bank and products and services desired by the consumer. This lack of consumer sensitivity leads to the paradox of efficiency in consumer banking.

Exhibit 9-1
Combining Efficiency and Effectiveness

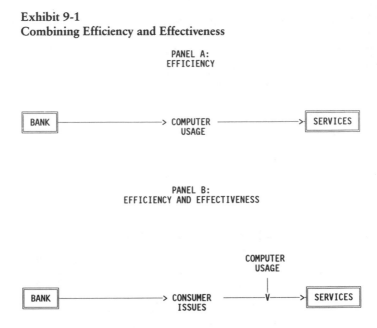

The Paradox of Efficiency in Consumer Banking

Banks' lack of consumer sensitivity stems from failure to define their mission. They are not only in the business of providing credit, but they are also in the business of marketing financial services (Metzger 1989a). Marketing financial services requires "a detailed knowledge of the market place, customer profiles, customer expectations, and the ability to provide consumers with the products and services they need, quickly and with a minimum of inconvenience" (Metzger, 1989a, 74). In other words, the banking industry needs to develop a much more consumer-satisfaction-oriented business rather than merely a "providing credit" business. However, primarily due to the industry's defining its mission as providing credit efficiently and profitably, banks have almost become obsessed with cutting down operating costs.

This emphasis on efficiency by cutting operating costs (Kranz 1988) has been facilitated by increased computer utilization. Banks have been using many different computerized systems in recording and communicating information ("If A Computer Answers, Don't Hang Up" 1989; "Technology: Impact, The Mechanization of Retail Banking" 1983; Violano 1988). In the early 1980s, much of the industry's development budget was spent on new computers and information systems as well as high-tech electronic fund transfer (EFT) networks (Metzger and Dey 1986).

Service charges were being increased at the same time traditional services were being decreased. In 1983, Citibank tried to move from human tellers for certain transactions by assessing consumers a service charge when they used the human teller for these transactions. Consumer activists reacted to this policy with a great deal of protest ("Technology" 1983). Retail consumers were not having their needs met. This particular development was not consistent with the banker's expected role in the consumer's life. This role always has been expected to be as personal as the consumer's relationship with a counselor, doctor, or lawyer. The aim of computerization has been to transfer consumer reliance from humans to machines (Haywood-Farmer 1984). In many cases, consumers are no longer communicating with the banker but with the computer through recorded messages (Kranz 1988; Violano 1988). With the computerization of banking and the depersonalization of the banker's role, the personal element of banking that was so important in developing such psychological ties as loyalty has diminished (Metzger 1989b; Metzger and Dey 1986; Sudo 1988a; Sudo 1988b). In any service industry, it is not depersonalization but personalization that yields the satisfactory results defined as consumer satisfaction and, therefore, profit realization. The banking sector is facing a paradox of depersonalizing itself for efficiency and, therefore, becoming less effective in providing consumer satisfaction. Banks must learn to appreciate the point that was made by Kelly Holthus, 1989 president of the American Banker's Association: "Take care of your people and the profits will take care of themselves" (Streeter 1989, 97).

An American Banker Corporate Survey indicates that the quality of service was the most important factor for a banking relationship (Sudo 1988b). One might assume without surveying consumers that cost would be a key service factor. In this study, cost ranked 10th in consumer relationships (Sudo 1988b). Therefore, cost, a key element of efficiency, is not the crux of consumer relationships.

The Kennedy Consumer Manifesto

The parameters have been set for developing consumer-friendly products and services since John F. Kennedy declared his consumer manifesto in 1963 (Kennedy 1963). According to the Kennedy manifesto, consumer satisfaction is defined as the right (1) to be protected, (2) to be informed, (3) to choose, and (4) to be heard. Although banks have made some progress in these areas, due to the increasing competition in the banking environment and such consumer regulations as the Truth-in-Lending Act, the Community Reinvestment Act, and Regulation CC of recent years, there is still much room to improve.

The four Kennedy conditions, although important, will provide only the basic services for the consumer, implying, at best, a consumer-neutral stage. However, in a competitive market system for services, the competitive edge is related to high credence qualities (Zeithaml 1981). The closer the consumer's perceptions of those services being delivered to those services that are desired, the higher is the credence. Since banks do not provide post-sale communication avenues for consumer feedback, they are not able to determine their credence qualities.

High credence is related to self-image/store (bank) image congruence (Samli and Sirgy 1981; Sirgy 1985; Samli 1989). The congruence concept implies that the way the individual consumer sees himself or herself is related very closely and positively to how the customer sees his or her bank. If the two are consistent, then the consumer feels good about patronizing that financial institution. Therefore, congruence would result in high levels of bank loyalty. In service industries, unlike the product industries, loyalty and high credence are related more closely to an individual's psychological needs.

High credence in banking cannot be achieved solely by satisfying the Kennedy conditions because there exist four gaps in service-related industries that need to be eliminated. These gaps are "(1) difference between consumer expectations and management's perceptions of consumer expectations; (2) difference between management perceptions of consumer expectations and service quality specifications; (3) difference between service quality specifications and the service actually delivered; (4) difference between service delivery and what is communicated about the service to consumers" (Zeithaml, Berry, and Parasuraman 1988, 36). These four gaps in the banking sector can be eliminated by meeting certain psychological needs of the consumer (Zeithaml, Berry, and Parasuraman 1988).

Psychological Needs of the Consumer

The bank must meet at least seven individual psychological needs (Exhibit 9-2) that will bring efficiency and effectiveness together in an effort to generate consumer-friendly financial services. In Exhibit 9-2, the banks' current behavior that manifests itself as a series of negative forces also is illustrated.

The seven psychological needs and the current corresponding bank behavior are (1) special attention versus robotic treatment, (2) advice versus sales pitch, (3) options versus minimum options, (4) quick reaction versus slow reaction, (5) understanding versus lack of acknowledgment or reassurance, (6) empathy versus nonpersonalization, and (7) information versus legalistic information and/or poor utilization of information.

Attention

Today's consumer, more than ever before, likes to be treated as a special person. Basically, it is an important part of the American culture to pay attention to the individual rather than the group or community. From the inception of the U.S. government as laid out in the Bill of Rights, concern has been centered around the individu-

Exhibit 9-2
Discrepancies between Consumer Needs and Bank Behavior

CONSUMER NEEDS:	BANK BEHAVIOR:
SPECIAL ATTENTION	ROBOTIC TREATMENT
ADVICE	SALES PITCH
OPTIONS	MINIMIZES OPTIONS
QUICK REACTION	SLOW REACTION
UNDERSTANDING	NO ACKNOWLEDGEMENT AND/OR REASSURANCE
EMPATHY	NON-PERSONALIZATION
INFORMATION	LEGALISTIC AND/OR POOR UTILIZATION OF INFORMATION

al's rights. Just as the psychiatrist, attorney, or doctor takes the time to listen, understand, and diagnose in an attempt to solve the individual's problems, the retail banker must be involved at the personal level with each individual.

Advice

Consistent with the special-attention factor, the banker will have to be able to render advice in a manner similar to a doctor or attorney. This particular advice must go beyond the efforts to sell. "If bankers do not know a consumer well, it may be because they spend less time on analyses than on selling" (Sudo 1988b). In the long run, advice that is most beneficial to the consumer will yield the most business for the bank. That is, if the banker can help a consumer perform better financially, the banker reaps the harvest of more profits.

Options

Closely related to attention and advice factors, the bank must have and should point out multiple viable financial and service options for the consumer. While from the view of computerized efficiency and the cost perspective, the minimization and standardization of the options may be desirable, the effectiveness criterion requires that consumers be given different and, perhaps, unique alternatives to a specific problem. If the consumer does not have a choice, chances are likely that he or she may seek solutions elsewhere (Gupta and Torkzadeh 1988).

Quick Reaction

Just as when a consumer visits a physician's office, frequently the visit to the bank implies a problem that needs to be resolved very quickly. The banker must realize that the pressure of the particular financial problem on the consumer may be as serious or even more serious than a symptomatic ailment that might take that person to the physician's office. However, much of the time the banks take relatively much longer to solve a problem than the physician.

Understanding

Consumers attribute some of their dissatisfaction with services to their inability to communicate their needs. If the hypothesis that consumers partially blame themselves for the dissatisfaction with the services purchased is correct (Zeithaml 1981), the bank's sensitivity to a consumer's psychological needs is essential for profit optimization. The bank should not understand only the consumer's need but, also, should contribute to the elimination of consumer's self-doubt rather than make a contribution to it. The bank can accomplish this through providing reassurance of the service's value to the consumer, as well as boosting the consumer's self-worth by eliminating cognitive dissonance (Walters and Bergiel 1989). Furthermore, the bank should not increase the consumer's self-doubt through improper information and lack of post-sale communications.

Empathy

Very closely related to understanding, *empathy* means seeing a problem through the consumer's eyes. This entails personalizing each consumer's problem and trying to cater to each consumer as if he or she is the specially important person that he or she actually is.

Information

Perhaps all of the six areas discussed above are related to information. If the banker does not have proper information about the consumer, the banker cannot pay special attention to individuals, cannot provide constructive advice, cannot offer reasonable options, and cannot react to the consumer's needs with understanding or empathy. Because of their overwhelming orientation to efficiency and, therefore, less personal services, banks simply do not have the proper information to provide consumer-oriented solutions for the individual. Thus, suboptimization on the part of the bank is a widespread occurrence.

The Current Practice of Banks

Unfortunately, the average bank does not meet the psychological needs of the consumer. In fact, as seen in Exhibit 9-2, the bank's treatment of the consumer intensifies the psychological needs. Exhibit 9-2 illustrates the current counterproductive behavior of banks. Although the following bank scenarios are fictional, they are representative of complaints recorded in surveys undertaken by the *American Banker* (Neustadt 1988; Sudo 1988a).

Robotic Treatment

Mr. S is standing in line for service. One teller has opened a window for service. The teller motions Mr. S to the window. The teller gives no greeting nor any personal acknowledgment. The transaction is completed in silence and Mr. S's receipt is pushed toward him. With a nod, Mr. S is dismissed. This lack of training in personal interactions results in a nonpersonalized and unfriendly impression upon Mr. S. This lack of personal attention does not induce loyalty by Mr. S to his bank.

Sales Pitch

Mrs. D has decided to use an equity loan. However, the amount on which interest is tax deductible is less than the total of the loan. Not realizing the nuances in the tax laws, Mrs. D deducts the interest on the total of the equity loan for her taxes. Later, during an Internal Revenue Service (IRS) audit, Mrs. D learns of this inappropriate deduction. If the lending officer of the bank had been concerned with meeting Mrs. D's needs and advising her on the best method to meet her needs instead of selling an existing product, Mrs. D would not be paying the IRS penalties.

Minimum Options

Mrs. M chose a bank because it had extended lobby hours on Saturdays. The bank changed its hours and now closes at noon. Since Mrs. M works on Saturdays, she is very frustrated about the new hours. When she discussed the situation with the branch manager, she was told that the corporate office, although realizing the amount of extended traffic on Saturdays, felt the cost savings to the bank outweighed any inconvenience their customers might experience. The bank's lack of emphasis on service options is likely to result in the loss of a profitable account.

Slow Reaction

A company needs to activate an advance on its preapproved line of credit in order to finalize a real estate transaction. The company's representative tries repeatedly to call the lending officer, but the phone is busy. She finally ceases trying to call and travels to the nearest branch. There she finds that the branch manager cannot approve the advance, so she must proceed to the main office where the lending officer who originated the line of credit is located. The lack of a monitoring system for the bank's technology, in this case the phone system, coupled with the bank's emphasis on centralization of authority, results in the inability to react quickly to meet the needs of a consumer. This inability to react quickly not only resulted in the customer's inconvenience but also in a substantial financial penalty due to the delay in the real estate closing.

Lack of Acknowledgment or Reassurance

Mr. J has had a recurring complaint about the inaccessibility and the inordinate length of time needed to gain access to his lock box. The bank, having studied the problem, instituted corrective action. However, not realizing the efforts by the bank to correct the problem, Mr. J leaves the bank prior to the institution's implementation of the corrective actions. The bank's lack of acknowledgment and reassurance to Mr. J of their appreciation for his constructive criticism and the reassurance that they would examine the problem resulted in the loss of a valuable customer.

Nonpersonalization

Mrs. J is the spouse of an active military man who is engaged in a life-threatening deployment. Due to anxiety over her spouse, Mrs. J forgets to deposit her check. As a result, funds for the checks Mrs. J has written are insufficient, and the bank has charged overdraft fees. Upon realizing the error, Mrs. J calls the bank and talks to the bank's representative. The representative refuses to refund any service charges even though the J's have had their account with the bank a number of years and the account has never been overdrawn. If the bank had its customers rated by value to the bank and/or information on age and prior overdrafts of an account, a bank representative could have contacted Mrs. J on this first-time overdraft and saved her the embarrassment of returned checks. The lack of empathy shown to Mrs. J during this trying time must have decreased her loyalty to the bank and is likely to result in negative word-of-mouth advertising.

Legalistic Information and/or
Poor Utilization of Information

Mr. K has a very large savings account and is quite independently wealthy. He has been banking with the same bank for over 20 years.

He needs some money quickly. The bank turns him down, insisting that, as a policy, it needs to run a credit check on all applications before approving a loan. This lack of information about a consumer coupled with the lack of flexibility available to front-line personnel to make an exception to a standard policy will result in the loss of a profitable customer. Also, bankers often poorly communicate information by using bank jargon and legalistic terminology in their conversations and written documents. All of these bank scenarios reflect a substantial degree of consumer insensitivity.

MANAGERIAL IMPLICATIONS

If the retail bank is not sensitive to the consumers' needs, the bank cannot optimize its performance, and consumers cannot receive satisfactory service. Banks, in their attempts to increase efficiency, are becoming depersonalized and, therefore, are losing their effectiveness. If efficiency and effectiveness are not balanced, the bank will suboptimize its profit. However, if the two could be balanced, then banks would provide the all-important customer satisfaction that, in turn, will improve the profit picture. Bringing efficiency and effectiveness together is neither an automatic activity nor a foregone conclusion. The bank must work at bringing these two together. We maintain that by satisfying the seven specific psychological needs listed in Exhibit 9-2 the bank may bring efficiency and effectiveness together, resulting in consumer-friendly financial services.

This consumer orientation, in essence, has two components. One component is to satisfy the Kennedy requirements. In doing so, the bank is brought to a consumer-neutral stage, meaning that the bank's services are, overall, minimally acceptable from a consumer perspective. The second component is catering to the consumer's psychological needs and eliminating the service gaps in banking. In doing so, the bank will be brought to a consumer-friendly stage and give itself a competitive edge in the consumer markets.

Of course, the fulfillment of the seven consumer needs implies that the banks must have a carefully developed consumer research activity and the resulting consumer databases. They will have to be involved in at least three types of consumer research activities. First, banks must have an idea as to what kind of image they are projecting currently. Second, they must understand the characteristics of their target markets and the self-image of their consumers. Third, they must be in a position to compare the first two activities and determine the necessary actions to create a congruence between the two; this also is referred to as high credence. Unless the seven psychological needs of the consumer are fulfilled, congruence is likely to be very low. Unfortunately, because of banks' emphasis on costs and lack of consumer orientation, they are not likely to pursue the high cost of starting an elaborate but necessary consumer research program.

With the internal cost-efficiency pressures that result in continuing depersonalization and the simultaneous external pressures for more consumer orientation, the banks need more emphasis on consumer behavior research. It is obvious that this research should be designed to meet the seven individual psychological needs of the consumer.

In this troubled era of banking, the combination of efficiency and effectiveness is perhaps the only avenue through which the banking sector can cope with the adversities that exist in the environment and establish a competitive edge. This optimization process is related to the overall performance of balancing its resources and market opportunities. Thus, becoming more consumer sensitive is not an option for a bank, but a necessity.

SUMMARY

The service industries are gaining more and more importance and power in our economy. Developing and offering services that are consumer friendly not only will make the service provider more successful and profitable but also will make the service seeker more satisfied. If the whole service sector develops such an attitude, then not only will both parties be more successful or satisfied, but the society as a total entity will benefit. In the first part of this chapter, the key aspects of developing consumer-friendly services are developed in general terms.

In the second part of the chapter, a more in-depth analysis of developing consumer-friendly financial services is presented. It is posited that the service provider must not depersonalize its service-producing activities in the name of efficiency. Unless those services are perceived to be correct ones and preferred by the service seekers, depersonalized, automated, and cost-effective financial services are not likely to be accepted by the market. In other words, if the service provider is not effective in providing the correct type of services, both provider and seeker will lose out.

REFERENCES

Bennett, David, and Mike Higgins. 1988. "Quality Means More than Smiles." *ABA Banking Journal* (June):46.

Gupta, Yash P., and Gholamreza Torkzadeh. 1988. "Re-designing Bank Service Systems for Effective Marketing." *Long Range Planning* (December):38–43.

Haywood-Farmer, John. 1984. "The Effect of Service Automation on Bank Service." *Business Quarterly* (Spring):55–59.

"If A Computer Answers, Don't Hang Up." 1989. *Nation's Business* (August):55.

Johnson, Frank P., and Richard D. Johnson. 1985. *Commercial Bank Management*. Chicago: Dryden Press.

Kennedy, John F. 1963. "Consumer Advisory Council: First Report." Executive Office of the President. Washington, DC: United States Government Printing Office, October.

Kranz, Kenneth. 1988. "Market Wise Technology, Customer Control Dial Up a Personal Touch." *Bank Marketing* (April):42–43.

Metzger, Robert O. 1989a. "The Banking Counterculture." *Bankers Monthly* (March):74.

Metzger, Robert O. 1989b. "Serving All the People All the Time." *Bank Marketing* (May):83.

Metzger, Robert O., and Sukhen Dey. 1986. "Affluent Customers: What Do They Really Value?" *Journal of Retail Banking* (Fall):25–35.

Neustadt, David. 1988. "Calling Officers Win Praise; Turnover Troubles Firms." *American Banker Corporate Survey* 33–37.

Samli, A. Coskun. 1989. *Retail Marketing Strategy*. New York: Quorum Books.

Samli, A. Coskun, and M. Joseph Sirgy. 1981. "A Multi-Dimensional Approach to Analyzing Store Loyalty: A Predictive Model." In *The Changing Marketing Environment: New Theories and Applications*, edited by Ken Bernhardt and Bill Kehoe. Chicago: American Marketing Association.

Sirgy, M. Joseph. 1985. "Using Self Congruity and Ideal Congruity to Predict Purchase Behavior." *Journal of Business Research* (June): 195–206.

Streeter, William W. 1989. "Ready for the Challenge." *ABA Banking Journal* (October):95–98, 101.

Sudo, Phillip T. 1988a. "Little Things Mean a Lot When It Comes to Service." *American Banker Corporate Survey* 23.

Sudo, Phillip T. 1988b. "Service Not Price is First Among Corporate Clients." *American Banker Corporate Survey* 15–18.

"Technology: Impact, The Mechanization of Retail Banking." 1983. *U.S. Banker* (June):71, 73.

Violano, Michael. 1988. "Should Computers Answer Your Bank's Telephones." *Bankers Monthly* (July):38–42.

Walters, C. Glenn, and Blaise J. Bergiel. 1989. *Consumer Behavior.* Cincinnati: South-Western Publishing Co.

Zeithaml, Valerie A. 1981. "How Consumer Evaluation Processes Differ between Goods and Services." In *Marketing of Services*, edited by J. H. Donnelly and William R. George. Chicago: American Marketing Association.

Zeithaml, Valerie A., Leonard L. Berry, and A. Parasuraman. 1988. "Communication and Control Processes in the Delivery of Service Quality." *Journal of Marketing* (April):35–48.

Zeithaml, Valerie A., A. Parasuraman, and Leonard L. Berry. 1985. "Problems and Strategies in Service Marketing." *Journal of Marketing* (Spring):33–46.

10 | Developing Environment-Friendly Products

INTRODUCTION

When Lord Keynes stated that "in the long run we will all be dead," it is doubtful that he had in mind a melanoma caused by the sun's rays, leukemia caused by radiation, or asbestosis caused by asbestos used in construction materials. This list can be expanded substantially. Humans, with only about a 75-year life span, have managed to create nuclear waste with a life span of 100,000 years. Deterioration of the environment not only is causing deaths but also deterioration of the human race by substantially increasing birth defects as well as affecting human well-being in such different ways as environmental allergies that are considered serious to the health of human body and human mind.

As new products become more complex with multiple inorganic components, the increasing danger to the environment and therefore human well-being also is increasing. It must be realized that marketing has multiple interests in this total picture. First, marketing is partially, if not fully, responsible for the emergence of new products. As they are diffused in the marketplace, marketing is causing partially or fully the environmental problems that are likely to interfere with the advancement of the quality of life (QOL) in the society. This leads to the second interest of marketing in the environmental picture. Marketing survives and flourishes as the QOL improves. If the environment within which the society exists deteriorates, the QOL, by definition, deteriorates as well. Thus, marketing's opportunities as well as its performance become questionable.

In this chapter, after exploring some of the major environmental threats and problems, a model is constructed to develop environment-friendly products.

THE THREATS AND PROBLEMS

There is much evidence that our natural resources are being exploited indiscriminately. As stated in a 1988 Environmental Protection Agency (EPA) report: "Waterways served as industrial pollution sinks; skies dispersed smoke from factories and power plants; and the land proved to be a cheap and convenient place to dump industrial and urban wastes" (EPA 1988a). Exhibit 10-1 presents information on the specific air pollutants that are being regulated. Many others are not being examined carefully or controlled at this point in time. These pollutants, unfortunately, are created by the production processes of thousands of products. They are, therefore, critical for marketing in its attempts to fulfill its mission of providing a better QOL for the society (Samli 1987; Samli, Sirgy, and Meadow 1987).

The environmental deterioration is caused by many products, which vary from spray cans with chlorofluorocarbons to nuclear energy that generates uncontrollable nuclear waste. While the chlorofluorocarbons are causing significant genetic changes or skin cancer by causing holes in the ozone layer, nuclear and other toxic wastes are causing a very substantial increase in birth defects and various forms of cancer (Mahon and Kelley 1987). It is estimated that toxic air pollution added up to 2.7 billion pounds per year (Easterbrook 1989).

The water we drink has constantly increasing levels of carcinogens; most of the foods we consume have DDT residue and other carcinogens present. Thus, unfriendly atmosphere is penetrating our bodies and causing some predictable and some unknown damage. There are thousands of dangerous chemical dumping places throughout the country. Cleaning these will run in the billions of dollars (EPA 1988b). Examples of hazardous waste generated by industry are given in Exhibit 10-2. Again, these wastes are generated as many products are being produced by the industry.

In June 1989, there were almost 2000 superfund sites that needed

Exhibit 10-1
Health Effects of the Regulated Air Pollutants

Criteria Pollutants	Health Concerns
Ozone	Respiratory tract problems such as difficult breathing and reduced lung function. Asthma, eye irritation, nasal congestion, reduced resistance to infection, and possibly premature aging of lung tissue.
Particulate Matter	Eye and throat irritation, bronchitis, lung damage, and impaired visibility.
Carbon Monoxide	Ability of blood to carry oxygen impaired. Cardiovascular, nervous, and pulmonary systems affected.
Sulfur Dioxide	Respiratory tract problems, permanent harm to lung tissue.
Lead	Retardation and brain damage, especially in children.
Nitrogen Dioxide	Respiratory illness and lung damage.

Hazardous Air Pollutants	
Asbestos	A variety of lung diseases, particularly lung cancer.
Beryllium	Primary lung disease, although also affects liver, spleen, kidneys, and lymph glands.
Mercury	Several areas of the brain as well as the kidneys and bowels affected.
Vinyl Chloride	Lung and liver cancer.
Arsenic	Causes cancer.
Radionuclides	Causes cancer.
Benzene	Leukemia.
Coke Oven Emissions	Respiratory cancer.

Source: U.S. Environmental Protection Agency, *Environmental Progress and Challenge*, U.S. Environmental Protection Agency, Washington, DC, EPA 230-07-88-033, August 1988, 7.

Exhibit 10-2
Types of Hazardous Waste Generated by Industry

Industry	General Waste Description
Chemical	Contaminated waste waters, spent solvent residuals, still bottoms, spent catalysts, treatment sludges, filter sludges.
Fabricated Metals	Electroplating wastes, sludges contaminated with metals cyanides, degreasing solvents.
Electrical Equipment	Degreasing solvents.
Petroleum Refinery	Leaded tank bottoms, drop oil, emulsion solids, API separator sludge.
Primary Metals	Pickle liquor, sludge with metal contaminates.
Transportation Equipment	Degreasing solvents, metals, sludges.
National Security	All types of wastes.
Other	All types of wastes.

Source: U.S. Environmental Protection Agency, *The Waste System*, U.S. Environmental Protection Agency, November 1988, 1–6.

to be cleaned up. Their number is likely to keep increasing until a very serious cleanup activity is authorized. Average estimated cost for the cleanup process is $21 million. Underground storage tanks are creating another major problem. Approximately 80% of these are constructed of unprotected steel. They are likely to rust and allow gasoline to seep through land and pollute the land and water. The cleanup process will take $1 million per spill. In addition to very serious health hazard considerations, the cleanup process itself is an extreme cost burden to the society. Spending large sums on such activities will make it more difficult for the society to improve its economic well-being. All these monies could have been saved and used for the enhancement of the QOL if the products had been evaluated before they were produced and distributed.

On the other side of the coin, more and more products are using more and more of our scarce resources in such a way that many of these resources soon may be depleted completely. Such industries as plastics, building materials, and supplies are using inorganic materials that cannot be replenished. Similarly, such industries as paper and construction materials are using too much wood and forcing our forests to shrink, causing much ecological imbalance, which in turn causes genetic and biological changes and mutations. This is simply a brief profile of a much deeper and untold story. If the society does not reverse some of the deeply rooted practices, our slow but definite self-destruction pattern is likely to continue. Once that happens, it may eventually no longer be possible to reverse our direction. In the meantime, not only private litigations and government penalties but primarily the cost of pollution due to banks being hesitant to extend credit or charge higher interest is costing the industry excessive sums in the short run (Kopitsky and Betzenberger 1987; Bergsman 1989).

Marketing has a two-fold interest in this process. First, if the markets get into a self-destructive mode, marketing will lose its raison d'être, which is facilitating exchange as well as enhancing the QOL (Samli 1987). Second, marketing is responsible for the creation and distribution of the products that eventually could cause the demise of the society and, indeed, of the world. Although there has been strong literature on consumerism from an environmental safety perspective (Day and Aaker 1982), the marketing literature is very limited. In a sense, this may reflect the overemphasis by marketing in the 1960s, 1970s, and 1980s on caveat emptor. With the advance of consumerism, it was claimed that the emphasis shifted to "caveat vendor"; however, this somehow did not go far enough to find some alternatives to ever-increasing environmental problems (Day and Aaker 1982). Because of its unique involvement in the increasing environmental threat, marketing must take a more responsible posture. It must generate environment-friendly products.

THE NEED FOR ENVIRONMENT-FRIENDLY PRODUCTS

In order to understand the need for environment-friendly products, it is necessary to understand the key issues. At least two key issues must be considered in dealing with the environment. The first is pollution and the second is depletion. Both of these are extremely critical issues. We consider these issues individually.

Pollution

Pollution in recent years may be considered as a new twist on one of Mark Twain's famous sayings: Everybody is talking about pollution but nobody is doing anything about it. Pollution of the environment is occurring in three areas: the air, the water, and the land. The air pollution is caused by many products. However, the most common and the most offensive still is considered to be the automobile. The air pollution in some cities, such as Los Angeles, has reached such proportions that it has been long estimated that living in Los Angeles, for a nonsmoker, is equal to smoking about two packs of cigarettes daily. While on one hand pollutants from factories, vehicles, and chemicals are polluting the atmosphere, other chemicals, as mentioned earlier, also are causing the thinning and, subsequently, even the destruction of the ozone layer. Without this atmospheric phenomenon, it will be impossible to survive on our planet.

Pollution of water has at least two separate dimensions: the seas and springs and other sources of drinking water. Although we consider ours an advanced civilization, we have not yet found a proper way of treating sewage. In most parts of the world, raw sewage is dumped into oceans in such volume that some parts of the world's seas cannot replenish themselves ecologically. Thus, sea life and a major source of our oxygen is endangered. This is without considering the fact that we have been dumping nuclear waste into our oceans for the past 30 years; if the containers in which the waste is stored do not last, a catastrophe may occur.

The water we drink, in almost all parts of the United States, has more dangerous pollutants than the safety standards prescribe. Again, discharging industrial waste into rivers has caused much of this pollution. Thus, drinking water is becoming a risk in terms of causing cancer and other diseases.

The land is being polluted perhaps at a faster pace than the oceans because consumers, particularly in industrialized countries, generate tremendous amounts of garbage. Again, just like the sewage problem, thus far we have not found good alternatives to the use of garbage dumps. In many parts of the United States, as the garbage production accelerates, we are running out of garbage dump sites. This is a focal topic in local TV and radio news programs. Neighborhoods are flatly refusing to allow the creation of dangerous chemical, industrial, and garbage dumps near them. However, there are already many industrial waste sites that are abandoned or neglected and are already a health hazard. They need to be cleaned up before another Three Mile Island or an even worse incident is experienced by the society. The cleaning of these sites is estimated to cost billions of dollars. From a marketing perspective, these monies would have been spent on goods and services, which in return would have enhanced the QOL in our society. Furthermore, the insecticides and pesticides that are used by farmers have reached levels that create health hazards by polluting both the air and the soil.

Depletion

All the metals and other related substances that are mined are depletable. Society's resources are not endless. What is more, much of these resources are depleted to a point of no return. Although oil prices, for instance, in the short run go up and down, unless we make holes in our valuable beaches, oceans, and forests, the world's fossil fuel reserves are estimated to last only another 20 or 30 years. There is still coal in the United States that could last around 100 years, but what is 100 years in the endless flow of time? Some of the precious and industrially important metals and substances are becoming very scarce. In addition, the world's wood resources are being diminished at a very fast pace. From the rain forests of the Amazon to the redwood forests of California, there is an alarming trend of receding forest borders.

It also must be considered that the closer we get to depletion of metals, fossil fuels, and other scarce resources, the greater are the pollution levels. Some metals, such as lead or mercury, and fossil fuels, such as coal, are very environment unfriendly. Constant exposure to high levels of lead creates multiple diseases, including brain damage among children. Mercury poisoning, again, can cause diseases and death among humans as well as animals and fish. Coal burning emits sulphur, which essentially becomes acid rain that is destroying plants, forests, and other living things.

THE PROBLEM

As seen from our discussion, the entropy in the environment already is noticeable and our prevailing consumption patterns primarily are accelerating it. The fact is that this trend can continue and can accelerate to the point of destruction. Marketing is playing a critical role in this process. However, unless marketing takes a proactive position, its role is likely to be negative in the deterioration of our environment.

Although in recent years we have made some progress in the direction of consumer protection, consumer education, and consumer information, not much progress has taken place in the area of environmental issues. Consumerism activity has stemmed from consumer complaints. These complaints are registered by many individuals as well as many consumer groups. As the number of complaints from individuals increases, many consumerist groups have emerged. Furthermore, during the past 25 years or so, every state in the country has developed an office of consumer affairs. These offices and other consumerist organizations pressure the business sector and the legislative bodies to generate some consumer protection, consumer information, and consumer education activity. However, it must be reiterated that these events have taken place in a reactive mode. In other words, they came about because of outside pressures.

THE REACTIVE NATURE OF THE MARKET

The market always reacts. Therefore, it does not make provisions for the future and is never proactive. When the Bon Vivant soup killed numerous people from botulism, the soup was discontinued after the fact. Thalidomide was banned after having created hundreds of thousands of crippled babies. Red Dye No. 2 caused cancer before it was discontinued. In all of these cases and a multitude of others, the market and health authorities reacted. But, by the time the reaction came about, substantial harm was done. However, let us consider the example of a nuclear power plant. Yes, the market may react and the product may not be sold if it is no longer considered a good product. On the other hand, until this point, many nuclear plants have been sold. The nuclear waste that is generated by these plants could destroy the world. In such cases, the market's reactivity may be too late and the harm could be too substantial. Thus, in the case of environment-unfriendly products, relying on the free market's self-regulation is like playing Russian roulette.

Tremendous damage may take place any time and discontinuing the product after the fact is not the best solution.

Certainly, destruction or even deterioration of the market is not wise from a marketing perspective. Marketing exists to serve the market and see to it that the QOL is improving in the society as a whole. Accelerating the environmental entropy, therefore, is hardly in the best interest of marketing. Even if they are not immediately destructive, environment-unfriendly products generated and distributed by marketing are bound to be excessively costly to the society in the long run. Thus, the necessity of generating environment-friendly products stems, at least partially, from marketing's becoming more long-run oriented and more proactive in assessing the environmental impact of products.

THE NEED FOR FUTURISTIC ORIENTATION

It is a repeating scenario that American business has become too short-run oriented. In fact, some people blame the marketing concept for this (Hayes and Abernathy 1980; Bennett and Cooper 1981). They maintain that emphasizing nonprice competition and catering to immediate needs of the market have made American firms extremely short-run oriented. Furthermore, in some industries, companies are so anxious to introduce the product quickly to the market that they do not do enough research to find out what the side effects of the product are likely to be. Dalkon Shield intrauterine devices (IUDs) caused cancer of the uterus, and Rely tampons created a big scare by causing toxic shock syndrome.

It is maintained here that in many cases the long-run cost, based on environmental impact or health disorders or other problems caused by products, would outstrip short-run benefits. Therefore, all products must be examined for their short- and long-run impact on the environment and they all must be assessed on the basis of their cost-benefit characteristics. The position that is taken in this chapter is that the cost of waste and pollution caused by environment-unfriendly behavior is very excessive. This cost is not contributing to companies' profits and certainly is reducing the QOL that marketing could and should deliver. In fact, in developing a new product that is environment friendly, it is necessary to develop a social cost theory. In developing new products, all the cost estimates are private costs. They do not include environmental risks or damages. However, in order to develop environment-friendly products, both public and private costs must be considered up front. This may help eliminate some extremely environment-unfriendly products before they reach the market.

NEED FOR PROACTIVE BEHAVIOR

Instead of waiting to see if something will go wrong with the product or some unexpected problem will occur, environment-friendly product generation necessitates proactive behavior. This proactive behavior will evaluate environment friendliness of all products and intercept those that appear to be unfriendly early on before a product causes any problems. Proactive evaluation of products must coincide with the concept-testing stage of the product idea decay curve (Kotler 1988). In other words, proactive evaluation of the new product idea must take place at the earliest possible stages of the product development process. Certainly by the time product specifications are identified, there will be a good opportunity to evaluate the product's environmental impact. Even though there have been attempts by lending institutions to evaluate company risks through the development and use of environmental audits (Scagnelli and Malloy 1987; Margolis and Lehner 1988), almost nothing has been done to evaluate products before they become a reality. If such an effort were to take place, at least four areas need to be considered: pollution, dangerous waste, recycling, and replenishment.

It is important to determine if a product pollutes air, water, or soil. Whether any of these is being polluted and to what extent must be resolved. Furthermore, it must be decided if the pollution rate will increase or decrease in time.

Dangerous waste created by products is not considered often. The Babcock and Wilcox company still is selling nuclear energy plants without having found a solution to nuclear waste. Carbon dioxide emission from automobiles has gone down per vehicle, but since there are many more cars on the highways, the total volume that is being emitted has continued to be on the rise. It is important to design products to minimize the use of hazardous chemicals and to minimize the production of hazardous waste.

Recycling is important on two accounts. First, it will cut down the waste and, second, it will reduce pollution and increase production efficiency. Recycling generally takes two different forms. First, recycling may occur in the production of the same product. For example, recycling automobile scrap steel to make more cars is basically the main process in auto making in Japan. The second recycling process is developing other products from relatively less dangerous waste. Three very interesting examples were given in the recent national news: recycling glass into *glassphalt* to be used for road construction, using ash from incinerated garbage to develop cement blocks, and recycling plastic soft drink containers to make carpeting.

Replenishment implies emphasizing organic and replaceable chemicals and materials to be used in the production of products. This sustainable use of natural resources means more emphasis on water, soil, and forest. Nonrenewable resources need to be used more carefully for such more important purposes as the high-tech, bio-tech, or pharmaceutical industries. In order to facilitate the proposed proactive behavior, there must be an instrument to evaluate products before they are marketed in large quantities. This reactive group of activities represents some progress but is hardly satisfactory, as discussed in Chapter 3.

The key problem with the area of environmental issues is that large numbers of consumers are not making enough of an issue and consumerist organizations are not necessarily occupied with environmental issues. Furthermore, the industrial sector has an extremely strong lobby that attempts to block (most of the time successfully) environmental legislation that will cost money to the industrial sector. Thus, the environmental area is perhaps more critical and more neglected in the total social responsibility arena. Perhaps the most important factor causing this shortfall is that the market does not plan for the future, it only reacts.

DEVELOPING ENVIRONMENT-FRIENDLY PRODUCTS: A MODEL

There are many new product development models. One such model is used here for illustration purposes (Samli, Sirgy, and Meadow 1987). The purpose here is not to discuss the merits or the specific steps involved in the model. Instead, the necessary environmental assessment activities are emphasized.

Exhibit 10-3 illustrates this model. The dotted lines are the environmental issues that are inserted in the original model.

The model begins with idea generation. Typically, all models follow this step with screening activity; however, a different position is taken here. Perhaps even before the internal feasibility is assessed, environmental feasibility must be evaluated in general terms. If, for instance, the proposed product, say an insecticide, appears to be too dangerous environmentally, the idea may be abandoned very early in the process. Once screening takes place and internal feasibility is established, environmental safety features need to be specified. Later on as the product is developed, environmental cost (or

Exhibit 10-3
Developing an Environment-Friendly Product

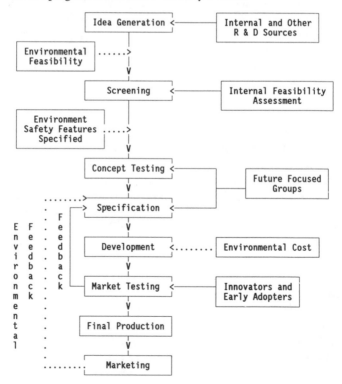

social cost) must be estimated. Again, if this cost is extremely high, the product will be abandoned before it is too late.

Finally, as the product reaches the market, feedback activity needs to continue. It is possible that there may be additional and unpredicted environmental effects that need to be stopped or the product will be recalled. The environmental feedback along with regular market feedback provides a solid foundation for future generations of the same product or for other products to be environmentally friendly.

In order to operationalize this model, American managers must become cognizant of the need for a strong environmental orientation (Post 1990). Such an orientation will also help further develop the economy (Mentzer and Samli 1981). Unlike all the recent objections to environmentalism on the basis of losing jobs, it is maintained here that this orientation will create many new and important jobs.

Much needs to be done in developing techniques or procedures to assess environmental feasibility, to identify environment safety features, and to calculate environmental cost of a proposed product. However, without these skills it is inconceivable that environment-friendly products can be developed.

SUMMARY

This chapter discusses one of the most important issues that will become a focal point in modern marketing: the development of environment-friendly products.

It is posited that environment-unfriendly products are becoming extremely costly to the well-being of the society and the prevailing QOL. Different aspects of air, water, and soil pollutions are discussed and problems that prove to be very costly are examined. The cost of pollution and elimination of the harm caused by pollution is more costly than intercepting the product at the beginning before it becomes an environmental menace. The estimated cost of cleaning air, water, and soil is so excessive that it probably will cause a net reduction in the existing QOL. A model is presented as an example to illustrate how the environmental impact of new products could be assessed early on, so that a devastating aftermath can be avoided.

REFERENCES

Bennett, R. C., and R. G. Cooper. 1981. "The Misuse of Marketing: An American Tragedy." *Business Horizons* (November–December):51–61.

Bergsman, Steve. 1989. "Banks Swamped in Toxic Wastes." (March):27–31.

Day, George S., and David A. Aaker. 1982. *Consumerism*. New York: The Free Press.

Easterbrook, Gregg. 1989. "Cleaning Up." *Newsweek* (July 24):27–42.

Environmental Protection Agency. 1988a. *Environmental Progress and Challenges: EPA's Update*. Washington, DC: U.S. Environmental Protection Agency, EPA/230-07-88-033, August.

Environmental Protection Agency. 1988b. *Office of Solid Waste and Emergency Response: Annual Report*. Washington, DC: U.S. Environmental Protection Agency, EPA/68-01-7259, November 1.

Hayes, R. H., and W. J. Abernathy. 1980. "Managing Your Way to Economic Decline." *Harvard Business Review* (July–August).

Kotler, Philip. 1988. *Marketing Management*. Englewood Cliffs, NJ: Prentice-Hall.

Kopitsky, Jerry J., and Errol T. Betzenberger. 1987. "Should Banks Lend to Companies with Environmental Problems." *The Journal of Commercial Bank Lending* (July):3–13.

Mahon, John F., and Patricia C. Kelley. 1987. "Managing Toxic Wastes—After Bhopal and Sandoz." *Long Range Planning* (August):50–59.

Margolis, Joshua, and Kevin Lehner. 1988. "The Environmental White-Globe Test: An Essential Management Tool." *Management Review* (September):44–48.

Mentzer, John T., and A. Coskun Samli. 1981. "A Model for Marketing in Economic Development." *The Columbia Journal of World Business* (Fall).

Post, James E. 1990. "The Greening of Management." *Issues in Science and Technology* (Summer): 68–72.

Samli, A. Coskun. 1987. "Introduction." In *Marketing and the Quality-of-Life Interface*, edited by A. Coksun Samli, xv–xviii. New York: Quorum Books.

Samli, A. Coskun, M. Joseph Sirgy, and H. Lee Meadow. 1987. "Measuring Marketing Contribution to Quality-of-Life." In *Marketing and the Quality-of-Life Interface*, edited by A. Coskun Samli, 3–14. New York: Quorum Books.

Scagnelli, John M., and B. Charles Malloy. 1987. "Should Lenders Require Environmental Audits?" *The Journal of Commercial Bank Lending* (July):14–19.

11 | The Changing Economic Power Structure and Marketing

As the economic balance in the marketplace changes, the consumers may become powerless. If the consumers cannot have a reasonable selection of products and services, they cannot enhance their quality of life (QOL). This situation will not be conducive for the society to achieve higher QOL standards for all. Assuming the consumer is capable of making at least some reasonable decisions in terms of choosing the most desirable goods and services, there will be a major problem if the economic balance is not changing in favor of the consumer. If the consumer is handicapped economically, educationally, or psychologically, then the problem is substantially more critical. In this chapter, after examining the changing economic balance, its impact on the consumer is discussed. Then, the relationships between the economic and political democracies are considered. Finally, the social responsibilities of marketing under these circumstances are examined.

THE CHANGING ECONOMIC BALANCE

As mentioned in Chapters 1, 2, and 4, the economic balance is changing in the American market. This change is reflected in at least three major factors: income distribution, concentration of economic power, and concentration of information power.

Income Distribution

Although politicians and some economists make a case for the statement that "there are typically fewer people under the poverty threshold as compared to, say, three years ago," this does not mean much because of inflation. Poverty thresholds do not lead but, rather, they follow inflation. Assume, for instance, the poverty threshold is $10,000, and there are 10 million people below this threshold today. With an average of 5% inflation a year and 1.5% population increase (assuming the number of poor is increasing proportionately to the total population), in three years the number of the poor will go down to approximately 8.5 million. This is simply because the poverty threshold has not kept up with inflation. However, in reality, income distribution has not been very good in our society and is becoming worse. For instance, it has been estimated that less than 5% of the American population receives over 16% of the total income. Similarly, the top 20% of the population receives more than 40% of the total income and this share is growing (Exhibit 11-1). This top-heavy income distribution has not changed much over the years. It simply has gotten a little worse. For instance, Phillips (1991) states that the combined net worth of the 400 richest Americans has trebled from $92 billion in 1982 to $270 billion in 1989. During the same time, the median family income just barely kept

Exhibit 11-1
Percent of Aggregate Income Received by U.S. Families

	1955	1960	1965	1970	1975	1980	1987
Lowest Fifth	4.8	4.9	5.3	5.4	5.4	5.1	4.6
Second Fifth	12.2	12.0	12.2	12.2	11.8	11.6	10.8
Middle Fifth	17.7	17.6	17.6	17.6	17.6	17.5	16.9
Fourth Fifth	23.7	23.6	23.7	23.8	24.1	24.3	24.1
Highest Fifth	41.6	42.0	41.3	40.9	41.1	41.6	43.7
Top 5 Percent	16.8	16.8	15.8	15.6	15.5	15.3	16.9
	100.0	100.0	100.0	100.0	100.0	100.0	100.0

Source: Statistical Abstracts of the United States. Washington, DC: U.S. Department of Commerce.

ahead of inflation. Similarly, the top 1% of the population has increased its share of national income from about 8% in the early 1980s to 11–12% by the end of that decade. Exhibit 11-1 illustrates the dramatic discrepancy in the earnings of different groups in our society. These patterns have prevailed for more than 30 years.

In addition to these discrepancies in income distribution, a portion of the population that is larger than ever before is not working and is not receiving income. This is because they have exhausted their unemployment compensations and are so discouraged that they are not looking for jobs anymore. There is an increase of over 20 million during the past 10 years in the portion of the population that could be in the labor force but is not. A large proportion of these people is assumed to be unemployed involuntarily and are not looking for employment. They are discouraged workers who are not making a contribution to the economic well-being of the society. When the income-receiving versus non-income-receiving sectors of the population are contrasted, then it may be seen that the non-income-receiving sector is growing at a faster rate than the total population. Unfortunately, there are not too many readily available statistics to examine some of these finer economic points in our society. The only indication for this proposition is numerous estimations by the news media as to the numbers of homeless in major American cities.

Distortion in income distribution creates substantial losses for marketing. If those who are below the poverty threshold were to be brought to the mainstream market, they would purchase goods and services that they could not afford to purchase before. This will stimulate the economy, benefit the profit picture, and improve the overall marketing performance. On the other side of the equation, those people who joined the mainstream market lately would find that their QOL would improve without making anybody worse off. This implies a net gain for the society's well-being.

It is quite doubtful, however, if the negative direction of income distribution can be changed. Left as is, the market is not likely to work in this direction and remedy the situation (Dugger 1989).

By 1992, the income of the richest 5% of the population after inflation and taxes is likely to be increased by 60% percent in a 15-year period. The next "richest" quartile experienced only a modest gain in real incomes. The rest of the society experienced a decline in their real income ("The Rich Are Richer" 1991). These facts reinforce Dugger's (1989) contention that the market does not take corrective action.

Concentration of Economic Power

Concentration of economic power in the hands of a few businesses, banks, or people, is a very critical problem in a society. The greater this concentration, the greater is the vulnerability of the economic balance in the society. As the economic power concentrates in the hands of a few, there is no guarantee that the competitive nature of the market will prevail. Increasing economic power implies an increasing monopoly power, which, by definition, indicates a decline in competition. Declining competitiveness is likely to diminish consumer benefits.

In 1991, 5 of the nation's top 10 banks announced megamergers. In the appliance industry, while the top 5 companies controlled 79.8% of the market in 1985, the share of the top 5 in 1990 went up to 97.4% (Exhibit 11-2). Similarly, in the tire industry, the top 5 companies increased their market share from 57.6% in 1985 to 66.1% in 1990. The same picture prevailed in the software industry. The share of the top five companies increased from 55.6% in 1985 to 61.9% in 1990 (see Exhibit 11-2).

In recent years, there has been a merger and acquisition craze in the United States. These led to concentration of economic power. General conditions under which horizontal mergers take place, for instance, are very conducive to raising prices. Analysis indicates that any merger of this type that is not creating synergies raises prices (Farrell and Shapiro 1990).

In most cases, mergers and acquisitions are consummated for a variety of reasons other than marketing strengths (Hise 1991). If those strengths are not considered to be important, they are likely to decline or diminish. Once again, this situation is likely to cause deteriorating overall marketing activities and subsequently create less than the best conditions for the consumer.

Unlike earlier works (Galbraith 1958), recent works on oligopolies indicate coalitions in cooperative oligopolies. This implies that under certain market, demand, cost, and behavior conditions, coalitions among cooperative oligopolies are formed (Rajan 1989). Such coalitions are likely to bring these oligopolists closer to a

Exhibit 11-2
The Changing Market Concentration in Selected Industries

BANKING

1985 Ranking	Billions of Dollars
Citibank	$173.5
Bank of America	118.5
Chase Manhattan	87.6
Manufacturers Hanover	76.5
Morgan (J.P.)	69.3
Chemical	56.9
Security Pacific	53.5
Bankers Trust	50.5
First Interstate Bancorp	48.9
First Chicago	38.8
Total Assets	**$774.0**

44% of assets held by top 100
banks

1990 Ranking	Billions of Dollars
Citicorp	$216.9
BofA/Security Pacific*	195.4
Chemical/Manufacturers*	134.5
NCNB/C&S/Sovran*	116.5
Chase Manhattan	98.0
Morgan (J.P.)	93.1
Bankers Trust	63.5
Bank of Boston/Shawmut*	56.2
Wells Fargo	56.1
First Interstate	51.3
Total Assets	**$1,081.0**

46% of assets held by top 100
banks

*Asset values for pending
mergers based on combined
figures.

APPLIANCES*

1985 Ranking	Market Share
Whirlpool	32.0%
General Electric	22.7
White Consolidated Ind.	13.0
Maytag	7.7
Ratheon	4.4
Total Share of Top 5	**79.8%**

1990 Ranking	Market Share
Whirlpool	32.8%
General Electric	27.0
Electrolux/WCI	17.2
Maytag	14.6
Ratheon	5.8
Total Share of Top 5	**97.4%**

*Annual unit production of
washers, dryers, ranges, and
refrigerators.

Exhibit 11-2 (continued)

TIRES		SOFTWARE	
Worldwide Sales		**1985**	**Market**
1985	**Market**	**Ranking**	**Share**
Ranking	**Share**		
		Lotus Development	21.5%
Goodyear (U.S.)	20.0%	Microsoft	15.5
Michelin (France)	15.6	Ashton-Tate	10.5
Bridgestone (Japan)	8.5	Digital Research	4.3
Firestone (U.S.)	8.0	Micropro International	3.8
Pirelli (Italy)	5.5	**Total Share of Top 5**	**55.6%**
Total Share	**57.6%**		
		1990	**Market**
1990	**Market**	**Ranking**	**Share**
Ranking	**Share**		
		Microsoft	25.4%
Michelin (France)	20.0%	Lotus Development	12.0
Bridgestone (Japan)	16.4	Novell/Digital*	9.7
Goodyear (U.S.)	16.2	Word Perfect	7.5
Continental (Germany)	7.2	Ashton-Tate/Borland	7.3
Pirelli (Italy)	6.3	**Total Share of Top 5**	**61.9%**
Total Share	**66.1%**		
		*Pending mergers	

Source: Adapted and revised from "The Age of Consolidation," *Business Week*, October 14, 1991, 86–94.

monopolistic situation. This is because cooperating oligopolistic coalitions will prefer not to compete as much as cooperate. These coalitions can divide the markets easily and establish themselves as partial monopolies rather than being engaged in what is termed by economists as cutthroat competition. Once again, avoiding competition by oligopolies indicates that economic power is concentrating and, therefore, competition is declining.

Concentration of Information Power

Alvin Toffler (1990) stated that: "Knowledge itself . . . is . . . not only the source of the highest-quality power, but also the most important ingredient of force and wealth." He continued on, saying that "knowledge has gone from being an adjunct of money power and muscle power to being their very essence" (12). Toffler equates the power shift in the society to be revolving around knowledge. The basic ingredient of knowledge, particularly in marketing, is information.

In 1982, John Naisbitt posited that our society is moving away from an industrial society to an information society. Drucker (1989) stated that people with more information or with better access to information are accumulating more power, which is reflected in economic power. Thus, another way of concentration of power in our society is information. People (i.e., consumers) do not have equal access to information; only a few have ready access to much of the information, which, once again, is likely to threaten the already fragile balance in our economy. Since consumers do not have equal opportunity, it is reasonable that access to information and concentration of income distribution, are correlated quite highly. Those who have better means are receiving better education, and those who are better educated have more access to information. Thus, concentration of economic power and concentration of information power are in the same direction, and they mainly overlap.

Concentration of economic power coupled with information power is likely to create, more than ever before, a lopsidedness in the marketplace. The discrepancy between the poor and the rich really will become noticeable, and will reach all-time highs. This situation will mean huge losses for the society as a whole because an ever-enlarging proportion of the work force either will be idle or will be employed inadequately. Because the workers in this group simply do not have access to information, they are not well trained or educated and therefore they can handle only menial tasks. Since the earnings of this group will be going down, marketing will be losing very large profits and, conversely, will not be able to exchange the very large volume of goods and services that would have been exchanged otherwise. The economic base of the society will shrink. The end result will be a decline in the QOL that is prevailing in the society.

In addition to the distorted income distribution, concentration of economic power and concentration of information power, there is an additional and very critical factor affecting the changing economic balance. This is termed here as the *second democracy*.

THE SECOND DEMOCRACY

While the first democracy is one person, one vote, the second democracy means one dollar, one vote. The critical feature of the democratic society is that these two democracies check and balance each other. The reinforcement of the two democracies indicates that consumers have a fair chance to become equal opportunity (not equal) consumers. In fact, only through the balance of these two democracies can the equal opportunity consumer concept be converted from a myth to a reality. This in turn means that marketing is being both efficient and effective in providing goods and services, not for a privileged few, but for all. In this way, an optimal QOL for the society as a whole almost is guaranteed.

Exhibit 11-3 illustrates this phenomenon. As can be seen, as the two democracies come closer together, the national economy experiences more and healthier competition. Increased competition leads to the emergence of a stronger equal opportunity consumer sector. As the two democracies completely overlap, all consumers are likely to become equal opportunity consumers. This situation leads to achieving an optimality in the QOL for the whole society.

However, as economic power has been concentrating in the hands of a few, economic democracy begins influencing the political democracy. This is when what Dugger (1989) called "the top dogs" benefit from the institutionalized status quo. They are enabled to believe that they benefit because of their personal talents or efforts rather than their greed, power, privilege, class, or status. If the market is deregulated and competition is not enforced, the two democracies start separating from each other. At the extreme, this separation can lead to a revolution in a society. It certainly is not quite correct to claim that the market system guards itself against such eventualities.

Thus, the greater the gap between the two democracies, the greater the chances of not optimizing the society's QOL. This is not in

Exhibit 11-3
Relationship of the Two Democracies

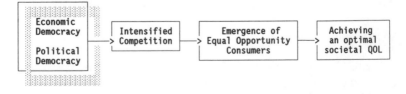

the best interest of the society in general and the majority of consumers in particular. Furthermore, it is not all in the best interest of marketing.

Although the distinction between the two democracies is reasonably clear, many authors combine the two and consider "consumer votes" to be the last word on the American democracy (Dickinson and Hollander 1989). If consumers' purchases were to be taken on their face value as "democracy at work," then it will not be possible to dissect economic power concentration and political power concentration. Thus, it will be almost impossible to consider a very large group of consumers to be equal opportunity consumers.

MARKETING IN ECONOMIC CONCENTRATION

This book begins with a statement that marketing is a very powerful social process that takes place in the market. As such, marketing can be used as one of the key instruments in gaining additional economic power. Through creative distribution, product design, pricing, and advertising, the firms and, therefore, individuals have a better chance of generating greater and greater revenues.

As oligopolies emerge, they become removed further and further from consumers than small competing firms. Oligopolies typically engage heavily in nonprice competition because typically price competition for them becomes a losing proposition, since none of the oligopolists can increase their market share or their profits by price cutting.

As Dugger states: "The market economy is a discretionary economy, a product of human will" (1989, 608). It can be changed through the collective action of consumers. Marketing could be instrumental in such a development. This may be an idealistic solution. However, any movement in this direction will benefit the society as a whole. In the presence of such a possibility and the possibility of everybody's becoming better off, organizations may stop their tendency to oligopolize. Even more than that, existing oligopolies easily can improve their profit pictures by helping more consumers to enter the mainstream American economy. Finally, oligopolies can pursue a low-price and far-reach policy in the marketplace and emphasize larger volumes of sales at lower prices with efficient and effective distribution. Selling proportionally higher volumes at lower prices rather than low volumes at high prices will increase profitability because the former will enable firms to take advantage of economies of scale and bring more people into the work force and the mainstream market. Far reach here is particularly important. It means efficient and effective distribution. Thus, enlightened self-interest on the part of the oligopolistic decision makers regarding their marketing decisions is likely to be beneficial to all parties involved (and/or concerned). These oligopolists easily can develop environment- and consumer-friendly products and services and can improve further the QOL prevailing in the society without any harm to the oligopolies or their companies. In the meantime, marketing continues with consumer education, consumer information, and consumer protection junctions that will improve consumers' chances of becoming equal opportunity consumers.

SUMMARY

A series of very critical considerations is discussed in this chapter. Above all, it is reemphasized that American competition is disintegrating and giving way to increasing economic concentration. The increasing economic concentration is related closely to distorted income distribution and lopsided distribution of information power.

As economic balance becomes more vulnerable, the relationship between the two democracies (i.e., economic and political democracies) also deteriorates. It is maintained in this chapter that these two democracies check and balance each other. As they become further apart, competition deteriorates and the number of equal opportunity consumers also declines.

Finally, marketing plays a critical role in the concentration of economic power. This role, however, could be reversed, and this could be beneficial for all parties concerned. It would provide a higher QOL for the whole society.

REFERENCES

Dickinson, Roger, and Stanley C. Hollander. 1989. "Consumer Votes." In
        Quality of Life Studies in Marketing and Management, edited by H.
        L. Meadow and M. J. Sirgy, 71–84. Blacksburg, VA: Virginia Tech.
Drucker, Peter. 1989. *The New Realities*. New York: Harper and Row.

Dugger, William M. 1989. "Instituted Process and Enabling Myth: The Two Faces of the Market." *Journal of Economic Issues* (June):607–615.

Farrell, Joseph, and Carl Shapiro. 1990. "Horizontal Mergers: An Equilibrium Analysis." *The American Economic Review* (March):107–125.

Galbraith, John K. 1958. *American Capitalism*. Boston: Houghton Mifflin Co.

Hise, Richard T. 1991. "Evaluating Marketing Assets in Mergers and Acquisitions." *The Journal of Business Strategy* (July/August):46–51.

Naisbitt, John. 1982. *Mega Trends*. New York: Warner Books.

Phillips, Kevin. 1991. *Politics of Rich and Poor*. New York: Harper Perennial.

Rajan, Roby. 1989. "Endogenous Coalition Formation in Cooperative Oligopolies." *International Economic Review* (November):863–876.

"The Rich Are Richer—And America May Be the Poorer." *Business Week* (November 18):85–88.

Toffler, Alvin. 1990. *Power Shift*. New York: Bantam Books.

12 | *Marketing Efficiency versus Marketing Effectiveness*

INTRODUCTION

Marketing efficiency has been a concern for scholars and practitioners for a long time. Whereas there has been some significant progress toward achieving greater marketing efficiency, marketing effectiveness issues are neglected almost completely. If the society improves its capabilities to deliver products and services efficiently but is not quite concerned about whom receives which product and services, the generated quality of life (QOL) is likely to be improved only for certain groups rather than for all. Furthermore, that society is most likely suboptimizing. Once again, marketing plays a significant role in this suboptimization or optimization process. This chapter explores the proposition that, if marketing brings efficiency and effectiveness together, it will generate greater QOL for all and it also will be benefiting itself.

EFFICIENCY IN MARKETING—
25 YEARS OF PROGRESS

Efficiency in marketing has followed two separate tracks. First is the area of logistics, which, during the past 25 years or so, has made phenomenal progress. Second are efficiency considerations in various functional areas of marketing, such as efficiency in retailing, efficiency in wholesaling, efficiency in channels of distribution, and so forth.

Efficiency in Logistics

During the past three decades or so, we have learned how to distribute goods and services efficiently. Efficiency is measured in terms of input-output relationships. We have learned to minimize the costs, to put together an optimal distribution system, to place warehouses in the most appropriate locations, to establish optimal levels of inventories, and to design the most desirable transportation systems. All of these developments resulted in reduced cost, reduced time, and reduced material waste.

Of course, in marketing, logistics efficiency is related primarily to reduced cost. Being able to handle physically the same volume of business at a lower cost and/or with minimum amount of resource utilization is basically a display of efficiency in physical distribution. Marketing has moved in this direction in a spectacular manner during the past three decades.

On the other side of the picture in function-related efficiency areas, retailers, wholesalers, and other related marketing intermediaries have shown significant efficiency improvements. Exhibit 12-1

Exhibit 12-1
Increased Efficiency in Marketing Intermediaries

Retailing Efficiency Measures	Wholesaling Efficiency Measures

• Merchandise Handling
   receiving
   delivery
   bulk breaking
	• Merchandise Handling
	   warehousing
	   automated order filling
	   large scale bulk breaking

• Inventory Controls
   minimized outages
   minimized inventory levels
   carried
	• Strategic Location of Inventories
	           minimum time for order deliveries

• Increased Sales per Salesperson	• Increased Efficiency in
	   Communications
	      reduced time between order taking
	      and deliveries

presents some of the key efficiency areas that have emerged in whole-saling and retailing during the past three decades.

Efficiency in Retailing and Wholesaling

As seen in Exhibit 12-1, the retailing sector has made major strides in merchandise handling. In receiving the merchandise quickly, delivering the merchandise on time to customers at lower costs, retailers' performance has been very impressive. Internally, merchandise handling is related to bulk breaking, packaging, and readying the merchandise for retail consumers.

The area of inventory control has become sophisticated substantially. Because of recent progress, retailers have minimized inventory outages that mean lost business. Furthermore, improved knowledge of inventory controls enabled the retailers to minimize the inventory levels that are carried by these stores.

Finally, through better store layouts and merchandise identification within the store, retailers have helped consumers to shop at their convenience through self-service. This automatically increased the sales volume per salesperson in the store.

Wholesaling, on the other hand, has made even more spectacular progress. Exhibit 12-1 illustrates some of the key areas in which wholesaling efficiency has been particularly notable. Three such areas are identified: merchandise handling, decentralized warehousing, and increased communication efficiency.

In merchandise handling, wholesaling has become very efficient, primarily because of improved and modernized warehousing facilities. These warehouses provide access to the merchandise within the warehouse and access to transportation outside of it. Automated order filling made wholesaling particularly efficient. Computerized order taking combined with conveyor belt merchandise handling has made American wholesaling quite successful (Samli 1990; Samli and Browning 1991). Finally, wholesaling has made special progress in receiving large volumes and breaking the bulk by making the merchandise ready for the use of retailers.

Decentralized warehousing has increased wholesaling efficiency by minimizing the waiting time for deliveries. Thus, the retailing sector benefits from reduced waiting time and increased efficiency.

Finally, somewhat related to the last point above, wholesalers' communication with retailers as well as with manufacturers has become very sophisticated. The net result of this sophistication has been a significant increase in communication efficiency, which, in return, reflects itself in advanced order taking and filling.

THE CONCEPT OF EFFECTIVENESS

Adel El-Ansary (1986), discussing problems in developing countries, brings the concept of effectiveness into focus by stating that poor consumers in the marketplace have special needs. The assortment of products they demand is limited to some very basic items. The lot size they demand is very small and the required delivery time is instant. El-Ansary further discusses moving from this effectiveness to efficiency through equity, which he elaborates on by stating: "This is the extent to which marketing channels serve problem-ridden markets and market segments" (47).

In the United States, however, the picture is reversed. Efficiency has superseded equity and effectiveness. Marketing has functioned quite well within the market mainstream. Efficiency in distribution has been achieved among the participants in the marketplace. However, emphasis on efficiency has left many consumers out of the market. This is due to the lack of effectiveness.

Effectiveness is defined here as the system's ability to deliver the specific products to specific groups according to the group's preferences. Current performance of the American distribution system in regard to effectiveness cannot be considered satisfactory.

From an effectiveness perspective, American marketing has not done very well. It must be noted that the markets that are left out of the total marketing and distribution process are not necessarily poor people without resources. Rather, because of ineffectiveness in the system, some market segments are left out. If these markets were to be brought into the mainstream, not only would marketing profits increase substantially, the outcome also will be enhancement of the existing QOL. There is much literature on distributor or manufacturer power in the overall distribution system (Butaney and Wortzel 1988; Hardy and Magrath 1988; and others). But it is hardly possible to find enough literature dealing with the role of customers (Butaney and Wortzel 1988). However, in many industries, customer power is substantial (or could be substantial). Bringing customers into the picture as key actors is not only consistent with the modern marketing concept but is also necessary from a profitable effectiveness point of view.

In such a situation, consumers will receive products and/or services as they deem necessary for themselves, rather than the manufacturer or distributor's making critical decisions for the consumer. Of course, in all cases, consumers will have access to products and/or services they may desire.

THE EFFICIENCY VERSUS EFFECTIVENESS DICHOTOMY

If one examines the current American scene, the effectiveness factor does not appear to be intact. Numerous industries perform less than adequately when their effectiveness is examined. On top of this list perhaps is the medical profession. While it is quite advanced and sophisticated, its outreach to the populace is quite poor. As this book is being written, the estimates are such that somewhere between 35 and 50 million Americans do not have access to medical services, nor do they have medical insurance. While these Americans are deprived of medical services, the health industry is operating with a large excess capacity. Many hospitals are empty, many health maintenance organizations (HMOs) can handle more patients and, above all, many insurance companies are not doing well. If these deprived consumers (who are not the very poor but who do not have access to Medicare) were to gain access to the medical industry, all parties likely would be better off. However, the industry needs to run itself based not on how much can the market bear but on the basis of what would it take to use the full capacity. The same types of analogies can be made in practically all American industries. While these industries are functioning at 60% or 70% of capacity, almost 10 million Americans are unemployed and many have given up looking for jobs and are not in the job market or in the marketplace as consumers. Furthermore, many Americans cannot afford to buy many of life's necessities because of their limited income and lack of access to products and services or because the products or services are expensive and the market system has been ineffective in designing cheaper and more adequate products and services for large groups of consumers with modest incomes.

The banking and finance sector is another critical industry. While many businesses and individuals cannot get credit to expand their businesses or improve their QOLs, the industry is plagued by careless and risky investments. Although it can lend substantially more, the industry simply will not lend money to those who need it. Thus, while the industry has much unused capacity, consumers' needs remain unsatisfied.

The airline industry is another example. While it has tremendous unused capacity, it has been raising prices. Thus, it has been discouraging consumers' use of the industry's services. Again, the industry's excess capacity remains unused while large groups of consumers' needs remain unsatisfied.

If the industries were to function at 95% or 100% capacity and if unemployment were to go to 2% or 3% (the Japanese have had even lower rates of unemployment; the United States also had lower unemployment rates many years ago), demand will be increased substantially. Simultaneously, if marketing were to increase its effectiveness, not only will consumers be better off, but marketing profits will be substantially greater.

Thus, in addition to improving its efficiency, if marketing were to provide cheaper and appropriate products and services for those who are at the periphery of the market, the QOL would be enhanced and so would the profit picture. The combination of efficiency and effectiveness is a must for marketing to function optimally in the society. Marketing can raise the society's overall well-being to a higher plateau.

These relationships are depicted in Exhibit 12-2. As seen in the diagram, efficiency and effectiveness working together and interacting will lead to optimal participation of consumers in the marketplace. This participation will yield a better QOL for all as it also improves the profit picture for marketing practitioners.

A PROACTIVE MARKETING PLAN

Efficiency and effectiveness interacting and working together is not a situation that is likely to materialize naturally and by itself. This may have been envisioned in Adam Smith's market (Smith 1779). Even then, there is doubt if this particular condition could

Exhibit 12-2
Efficiency and Effectiveness

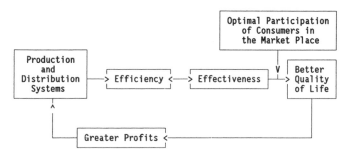

have become a reality in the marketplace. Undoubtedly, in today's market this situation will not take place through natural causes or market forces. Only a proactive marketing philosophy can make that happen. Throughout this book much of the discussion directly or indirectly refers to such a philosophy. Of course such a philosophy will prove its effectiveness only with the outcomes of its implemented proactive marketing plan. The key question at this point is: What are the key features of a proactive marketing plan that reflect the philosophy of raising the QOL by improving both effectiveness and efficiency of marketing simultaneously?

Such a proactive marketing plan is reflected in the concept of "value marketing," which is brought to the fore by *Business Week* ("Value Marketing" 1991). The key components of a value marketing plan are such that, if implemented properly, marketing's efficiency and effectiveness will be optimized, which in turn will optimize the QOL and the profits in the marketplace. However, this author maintains that any marketing is value marketing; the critical point here is optimizing the QOL and the profits simultaneously.

The proactive marketing plan, over and beyond assuming efficiency, has seven critical features that need to be discussed here. These are (1) offer products that perform, (2) give more than the consumer expects, (3) give guarantees, (4) avoid unrealistic pricing, (5) give the consumer the facts, (6) build relationships ("Value Marketing" 1991), and (7) penetrate the market.

1. Offer Products that Perform. Of course, the concept includes services also. Since the product or service is a bundle of utilities

(Kotler 1991), offering a product that performs implies satisfying the consumers' needs and providing them with optimum quality. The same consideration is applicable to services also. The proactive philosophy here should not be "give them any color they want as long as it is black," or "satisfy the consumers' needs," but it should be "let's delight our customers." In order to delight the customer, the first prerequisite is to offer a very good product or service.

2. *Give More than the Consumer Expects.* Attempting to delight the consumer goes beyond offering a good product or service. There must be a plus factor that the consumer did not even think of receiving. These may be environmentally sound packaging, including air conditioning in the car's standard price, free special delivery or free inspection for quality control, and many others.

3. *Give Guarantees.* Offering an enhanced and comprehensive warranty and paying full refunds without delay are critical features of a proactive marketing that aims to delight the consumers. From an accounting perspective, this may mean not a cost but an investment in the future of the business or the product.

4. *Avoid Unrealistic Pricing.* Companies should not think in terms of profit per unit. Charging premium prices may not be justified by the product. Furthermore, if pricing was to maximize the utilization of the firm's total productive capacity and hence optimize profits by selling the largest possible volume, not only the firm will receive handsome returns on investment but customers will receive great benefits from buying reasonably priced products.

5. *Give the Consumer the Facts.* Not only through advertising, but also through other means, such as labels, package brochures, and so on, provide consumers with valuable information that will enable them to make important purchase decisions. These decisions will enhance their QOL. Both today's sophisticated customer and today's confused customer need help to improve their purchase decisions. Therefore, they literally demand factual and detailed information about the products and services they are considering buying.

6. *Build Relationships.* Relationships mean repeat sales, which in turn imply product or brand loyalty. Good marketing means repeat sales. Any and all such devices as frequent buyer plans, 800 numbers, and membership clubs can help develop product and brand loyalty.

7. *Penetrate the Market.* Earlier in this chapter, efficiency was

considered a given before the components of the proactive marketing plan are discussed. However, over and beyond efficiency in distribution and logistics, there is still the effectiveness factor. Distributing products and services among those who need them the most as well as desire them the most is a critical consideration. As long as there are excess productive capacities and excess distribution as well as logistics capabilities, the firm must produce as much as possible and deliver all the output effectively (i.e., provide the proper product to those with specific needs). In carrying out this effectiveness concept, if the firm truly can penetrate the market to a point at which not only those who are the core of markets but also those who are at the periphery of the market will receive these products and services, all parties will be satisfied. This is what the true spirit of the marketing concept implies. There must be more for everybody at a reasonable profit.

SUMMARY

American marketing has made significant progress in improving its effectiveness. While this progress is due partially to progress in physical distribution, it also has benefitted from improved efficiency in various functional areas of marketing.

This chapter posits that if marketing becomes effective along with being efficient, it will provide an optimal participation of consumers in the marketplace. This optimal participation would enhance the existing QOL in the society as it also improves the overall marketing profit pictures.

In order to provide the desired optimal participation, a seven-point marketing plan is proposed. This plan is likely to be used by all marketers in all markets. The seven points are (1) offer products that perform, (2) give more than the consumer expects, (3) give guarantees, (4) avoid unrealistic pricing, (5) give the consumer the facts, (6) build relationships, and (7) penetrate the market.

REFERENCES

Butaney, Gul, and Lawrence H. Wortzel. 1988. "Distributor Power versus Manufacturer Power: The Customer Role." *Journal of Marketing* 88 (January):52–63.

El-Ansary, Adel I. 1986. "How Better Systems Could Feed the World." *International Marketing Review* (Spring):39–49.

Hardy, Kenneth G., and Allan J. Magrath. 1988. "Planning for Better Channel Management." *Long Range Planning* 21(6):30–37.

Kotler, Philip. 1991. *Marketing Management.* Englewood Cliffs, NJ: Prentice-Hall.

Samli, A. Coskun. 1990. "Wholesaling: Marketing's Forgotten Frontier." In *Developments in Marketing Science*, Vol. 13, edited by B. J. Dunlap, 203–207. Miami: Academy of Marketing Science.

Samli, A. Coskun, and John M. Browning. 1991. "Exploring Modern American Wholesaling: An Assessment and Research Agenda." In *Developments in Marketing Science*, Vol. 14, edited by R. L. King, 86–90. Miami: Academy of Marketing Science.

Smith, Adam. 1779. *Wealth of Nations.* London: George Routledge.

"Value Marketing." 1991. *Business Week* (November 11):132–140.

| *Epilogue*

This book deals with the social responsibility considerations in marketing. The position that is taken in the book is that socially responsible proactive marketing behavior not only is beneficial to the society but also is profitable to marketing. However, this kind of performance depends on a better understanding of the role marketing plays within the economy and society. On this basis, it would be possible to take a socially responsible posture that will enhance the quality of life (QOL) as it also yields greater profits.

If this premise is accepted and is operationalized, a very carefully designed research agenda must be developed and put in operation. Without such a research agenda, it is not likely that the envisioned social responsibility posture can be operative and able to yield the expected results.

The expected results in the operationalized socially responsible behavior are not immediate, and time must elapse before visible results can be detected. The role of research, therefore, becomes doubly important. Only through research can a tendency toward success or failure of proactive socially responsible marketing practices be detected before these policies have full impact. This way, it would be possible to intercept the policies that show an early tendency to fail. Research, therefore, leads to corrective action before it is too late.

Exhibit E-1 illustrates the areas of the research agenda that should be an integral component of the overall proactive marketing

Exhibit E-1
A Social Responsibility Research Agenda

> Consumer Satisfaction Issues

What do consumers need?
What are the specific differences among market segments?
What are the key consumer complaints?
Are products adequately consumer friendly?
Are the services adequately consumer friendly?

> Environmental Issues

How could a system of evaluation be established to assess environment
  friendliness?
How to develop a social cost system
Environmental impact feedback systems

> Consumer Protection Issues

How dangerous are the products? To whom?
How could the consumers be protected?
What kind of legislation is necessary?
What recourse do consumers have?

> Consumer Information Issues

Do manufacturers adequately explain the dangers of the product?
Where would consumers receive information?
Do the makers need persuasion to help consumers to protect themselves?
Is there proper labeling and other pertinent information?

> Consumer Education Issues

Do consumers receive enough information to make reasonable purchase
  choices?
How could the consumers be given better education to improve their
  decision making process?

Feedback

effort. As the exhibit illustrates, the research agenda in socially responsible marketing activity has at least five key areas of concentration:

1. Consumer Satisfaction Issues. Marketing cannot be effective and QOL cannot be improved unless consumers are satisfied. Consumer satisfaction is related closely to the way and the degree to which consumers' needs are met. This particular consideration cannot be operationalized unless marketing has very specific and powerful tools to segment the market sensitively and accurately. Consumer friendliness of the products and services is related quite closely to segments. Thus, consumer satisfaction research covers a major territory and delves into some very specific issues. It is envisioned here that one day marketing will be able to design and offer the exact products and services that are desired by very well-defined market segments.

2. *Environmental Issues.* Marketing cannot survive if the society does not survive. Hence, environmental issues are extremely critical. Perhaps the most important research agenda in this context is related to developing a technique by which the environmental friendliness (or lack thereof) of a product can be measured. Very closely related to this issue is the social cost accounting area. Research is necessary to determine the social cost of a proposed new product, along with its private cost estimates that are intrinsic to the firm and follow standard costing procedures. Since social cost accounting is not even born yet, we do not have any way of determining if the product is excessively costly for the society or not. Without having an approximation of the social cost of a proposed new product, it is not possible to determine its cost-benefit ratio and rationalize its production or elimination. Finally, a special feedback system is needed that monitors the product's environmental performance so that any errors at the early stages of a product's development will not cause an environmental disaster.

3. *Consumer Protection Issues.* As was discussed in Chapter 5, those consumers who are vulnerable particularly need to be protected so that they will be (or remain) equal opportunity consumers. Here, consumers need to be protected against the dangerous effects of certain products. For whom are the products particularly dangerous? It must be realized that smoking is particularly dangerous for those who have respiratory problems, as is alcohol to those who are alcoholics. The ways to protect the consumer and the kinds of legal constraints that are necessary for consumer protection are focal points of this research area. Presently, there are very few recourse options for consumers. Because of this, most consumers do not speak up and direct the firm and/or the system in the right direc-

tion. Developing consumer recourse is essential for effective marketing and for enhancement of QOL. This area requires much-needed in-depth research.

4. *Consumer Information Issues.* It is particularly critical that consumers are informed about the dangers of the product or the service. Much needs to be done in regard to determining if the manufacturers are providing enough information for consumers to protect themselves. Where consumers receive information about products and if that information is adequate are critical research areas that need to be cultivated. The outcome of such research is better communication with consumers that will reduce the burden of liability on the part of the makers and distributors of the products and services. How could the makers of products be persuaded to impart as much information about the product as possible? How much of this information should go along with the product itself in terms of labels, brochures, and so on? These, again, are critical research questions.

5. *Consumer Education Issues.* In the final analysis, if consumers have better education, they will be able to make more critical decisions and will tend to become more rational. Our society has done little, if anything, to make consumers more competent in their decision making. Consumer education goes well beyond providing the consumer with adequate information. It is related directly to developing skills to use information rationally for better decision making. The research question is to determine how consumers can be better educated so that they optimize their decisions. Their optimization will benefit the whole society.

Future research must point out if efficiency and effectiveness are coming closer and, hence, the society's QOL is approaching the point of optimization. In this context, marketing must find better ways of penetrating the market as far as the excess capacities and unused resources will allow. The current way of thinking, both in business and government circles, is far from this type of orientation. There are no known research tools to determine the proximity of efficiency and effectiveness or the intensity of market penetration in terms of existing unused capacities and resources.

Finally, Exhibit E-1 has a sixth point that is perhaps most critical. In all of the five research areas that are discussed above, there must be a feedback function that will report quickly on the activities of marketers and the results on the consumers and society. It is particularly important to determine preliminary impact of these functions by developing critical and effective early indicators so that quick adjustments can be made. The future of socially responsible proactive marketing depends on feedback. Without such a feedback function, corrective action cannot take place, and proactive as well as socially responsible marketing cannot become a reality.

Selected Bibliography

Aaker, David A., and George S. Day. 1982a. "A Guide to Consumerism." In *Consumerism*, edited by David A. Aaker and George S. Day. New York: The Free Press.

Aging America: Trends and Projections 1985-1986 Edition. Washington, DC: U.S. Government Printing Office, 1986.

Alderson, Wroe. 1957. *Marketing and Executive Action*. Homewood, IL: Richard D. Irwin.

Alderson, Wroe. 1965. *Dynamic Marketing Behavior: A Functionalist Theory of Marketing*. Homewood, IL: Richard D. Irwin.

Andreasen, Alan. 1976. "The Differing Nature of Consumerism in the Ghetto." *Journal of Consumer Affairs* (Winter).

Arndt, Johan. 1967. "Role of Product-Related Conversations in the Diffusion of a New Product." *Journal of Marketing Research* 291-295.

Assael, H. 1981. *Consumer Behavior and Marketing Action*. Boston: Kent Publishing.

Bartels, Robert. 1967. "A Model for Ethics in Marketing." *Journal of Marketing* 31 (January):20-25.

Bauer, Raymond A. 1967. "Consumer Behavior as Risk Taking." In *Risk Taking and Information Handling in Consumer Behavior*, edited by Donald F. Cox, 23-33. Boston: Division of Research, Graduate School of Business Administration, Harvard University.

Bauer, Raymond A., and Stephen A. Greyser. 1968. *Advertising in America: The Consumer View*. Cambridge: Harvard University Press.

Bennett, David, and Mike Higgins. 1988. "Quality Means More than Smiles." *ABA Banking Journal* (June):46.

Bennett, R. C., and R. G. Cooper. 1981. "The Misuse of Marketing: An

American Tragedy." *Business Horizons* (November–December):51–61.

Bernbach, V. S. 1962. "Is Advertising Morally Responsible?" *Yale Daily News* (Special Issue).

Bettman, James R. 1972. "Perceived Risk: A Measurement Methodology and Preliminary Findings." *Proceedings of the Third Annual Conference of the Association for Consumer Research* 394–403.

Bettman, James R. 1973. "Perceived Risk and Its Components: Model and Empirical Test." *Journal of Marketing Research* 10:184–190.

Bishop, James W., and Henry W. Hubbard. 1969. *Let The Seller Beware.* Washington, DC: National Press Inc.

Blattberg, R. C., and S. K. Sen. 1976. "Market Segments and Stochastic Brand Choice Models." *Journal of Marketing Research* 13:33–45.

Brody, R. P., and S. M. Cunningham. 1968. "Personality Variables and the Consumer Decision Process." *Journal of Marketing Research* 5:50–57.

Brown, G. 1952–1953. "Brand Loyalty—Fact or Fiction." *Advertising Age* (June 19, 1952):53–55; (June 30, 1952):45–47; (July 14, 1952): 54–56; (July 28, 1952):46–48; (August 11, 1952):56–58; (September 1, 1952):80–82; (October 6, 1952):82–86; (December 1, 1952):76–79; (January 25, 1953):75–76.

Brown, Vernon, Craig A. Kelley, and Ming-Tung Lee. 1991. "State-of-the-Art in Labeling Research Revisited: Developments in Labeling Research 1978–1990." In *Enhancing Knowledge Development in Marketing*, edited by Mary C. Gilly et al., 717–725. Chicago: American Marketing Association.

Bruner, J. S. 1957. "Going Beyond the Information Given." In *Contemporary Approaches to Cognition*, edited by J. S. Bruner, E. Brunswick, L. Festinger, F. Heider, K. F. Muenzinger, C. E. Osgood, and D. Rapaport. Cambridge: Harvard University Press.

Bruner, J. S., and C. D. Goodman. 1947. "Value and Need as Organizing Factors in Perception." *Journal of Abnormal and Social Psychology* 42:33–44.

Bruner, J. S., and L. Postman. 1948. "Symbolic Value as an Organizing Factor in Perception." *Journal of Social Psychology* 27:203–208.

Bruner, J. S., D. Shapiro, and R. Taguiri. 1958. "The Meaning of Traits in Isolation and in Combination." In *Person Perception and Interpersonal Behavior*, edited by R. Taguiri and L. Petrullo. Stanford, CA: Stanford University Press.

Bruner, J. S., and R. Taguiri. 1954. "The Perception of People." In *Handbook of Social Psychology*, Vol. 2, edited by G. Lindzey, 635–654. Reading, MA: Addison-Wesley.

Caplovitz, David. 1963. *The Poor Pay More*. New York: The Free Press.

Carson, Rachel. 1962. *Silent Spring*. Boston: Houghton Mifflin.

Cooper, Philip D., and George Miaoulis. 1988. "Altering Corporate Strategic Criteria to Reflect the Changing Environment: The Role of Life Satisfaction and the Growing Senior Market." *California Management Review* (Fall):87–97.

Davis, Mark A. 1989. "Establishing the Link between Nursing Home Costs and Nursing Home Quality." In *Quality-of-Life Studies in Marketing and Management*, edited by H. Lee Meadow and M. Joseph Sirgy, 289–290. Blacksburg, VA: Virginia Tech.

Day, George S. 1976. "Assessing the Effects of Information Disclosure Requirements." *Journal of Marketing* (April):42–52.

Day, Ralph, and E. Laird Landon, Jr. 1977. "Towards a Theory of Consumer Complaining Behavior." In *Consumer and Industrial Buying Behavior*, edited by Arch Woodside, Jagdish Sheth, and Peter Bennett. Amsterdam: North-Holland Publishing Co.

Dichter, Ernest. 1960. *The Strategy of Desire*. Garden City, NJ: Doubleday.

Dickinson, Roger, and Stanley C. Hollander. 1989. "Consumer Votes." In *Quality-of-Life Studies in Marketing and Management*, edited by H. L. Meadow and M. J. Sirgy. Blacksburg, VA: Virginia Tech.

"Do Good Ethics Ensure Good Profits?" 1989. *Business and Society Review* (Summer):4–10.

Drucker, Peter. 1989. *The New Realities*. New York: Harper and Row.

Dugger, William M. 1989. "Instituted Process and Enabling Myth: The Two Faces of the Market." *Journal of Economic Issues* (June):607–615.

Dychtwald, Ken. 1989. *Age Wave: The Challenges and Opportunities of an Aging America*. Los Angeles: Jeremy P. Tarcher, Inc.

Dyer, R. F., and P. G. Kuehl. 1978. "A Longitudinal Study of Corrective Advertising." *Journal of Marketing Research* 15:39–48.

El-Ansary, Adel I. 1986. "How Better Systems Could Feed the World." *International Marketing Review* (Spring):39–49.

Engel, James F., Roger D. Blackwell, and Paul K. Miniard. 1990. *Consumer Behavior*. Chicago: Dryden Press.

Environmental Protection Agency. 1988c. *Solid Waste and Emergency Response: The Waste System*. Washington, DC: U.S. Environmental Protection Agency, November.

Feldman, Lawrence P. 1971. "Societal Adaptation. A New Challenge for Marketing." *Journal of Marketing* 35 (July).

Ferber, Robert, and Lucy Chao Lee. 1974. "Husband-Wife Influence in Family Purchasing Behavior." *Journal of Consumer Research* 1 (June):43–50.

Ferrell, O. C., and John Fraedrich. 1981. *Business Ethics*. Boston: Houghton Mifflin.

Ferrell, O. C., Larry Gresham, and John Fraedrich. 1989. "A Synthesis of Ethical Decision Models for Marketing." *Journal of Macromarketing* (Fall):55–64.

Galbraith, John Kenneth. 1958. *The Affluent Society*. Boston: Houghton Mifflin.

Gaski, John F. 1985. "Dangerous Territory: The Societal Marketing Concept Revisited." *Business Horizons* (July–August):42–47.

Goodman, Charles S., and Thomas C. Fidandler. 1965. *Distribution in a High Level Economy*. Englewood Cliffs, NJ: Prentice-Hall.

Gupta, Yash P., and Gholamreza Torkzadeh. 1988. "Re-designing Bank Service Systems for Effective Marketing." *Long Range Planning* (December):38–43.

Hansen, Flemming. 1976. "Psychological Theories of Consumer Choice." *Journal of Consumer Research* 3:117–142.

Hayes, R. H., and W. J. Abernathy. 1980. "Managing Our Way to Economic Decline." *Harvard Business Review* (July–August):67–77.

Haywood-Farmer, John. 1984. "The Effect of Service Automation on Bank Service." *Business Quarterly* (Spring):55–59.

Hirschman, Albert O. 1970. *Exit, Voice and Loyalty*. Cambridge, MA: Harvard University Press.

Hirschman, Elizabeth C. 1983. "Consumer Intelligence Creativity and Consciousness: Implications for Consumer Protection and Education." *Journal of Public Policy and Marketing* 2:153–170.

Hise, Richard T. 1991. "Evaluating Marketing Assets in Mergers and Acquisitions." *The Journal of Business Strategy* (July–August):46–51.

Humphreys, M. A., and J. M. Kenderdine. 1979. "They've Even Made Him to Lawyers." Norman, OK: Working Paper Series No. 78-7, University of Oklahoma, Division of Marketing.

Hunt, Shelby. 1971. "The Morphology of Theory of the General Theory of Marketing." *Journal of Marketing* 35 (April):65–68.

"If A Computer Answers, Don't Hang Up." 1989. *Nation's Business* (August):55.

Jacoby, Jacob, Robert W. Chestnut, and William Silberman. 1977. "Consumer Use and Comprehension of Nutrition Information." *Journal of Consumer Research* (September):119–128.

Johnson, Frank P., and Richard D. Johnson. 1985. *Commercial Bank Management*. Chicago: Dryden Press.

Kassarjian, Harold E. 1986. "Consumer Research: Some Recollections and Commentary." *Advances in Consumer Research* 13:6–8.

Kelley, Eugene. 1963. "Ethical Behavior in Marketing." In *Toward Scientif-*

ic Marketing, edited by Stephen A. Greyser. Chicago: American Marketing Association.

Kennedy, John F. 1963. "Consumer Advisory Council: First Report." Executive Office of the President, Washington, DC: United States Government Printing Office, October.

Kotler, Philip. 1968. "Beyond Marketing: The Furthering Concept." *California Management Review* 12 (Winter).

Kotler, Philip. 1969. "A New Form of Marketing Myopia: Rejoinder to Professor Luck." *Journal of Marketing* 33 (July):55–57.

Kotler, Philip. 1972. "A Generic Concept of Marketing." *Journal of Marketing* (April):46–54.

Kotler, Philip. 1973. "A Generic Concept of Marketing." In *Social Marketing*, edited by W. Lazer and E. Kelley. Homewood, IL: Richard D. Irwin.

Kotler, Philip. 1979. "Strategies for Introducing Marketing into Non-Profit Organizations." *Journal of Marketing* 43 (January):37–44.

Kotler, Phillip. 1991. *Marketing Management*. Englewood Cliffs, NJ: Prentice-Hall.

Kotler, Philip, and Gerald Zaltman. 1971. "Social Marketing: An Approach to Planned Social Change." *Journal of Marketing* 37 (July):3–12.

Kranz, Kenneth. 1988. "Market Wise Technology, Customer Control Dial Up a Personal Touch." *Bank Marketing* (April):42–43.

Kuehl, Phillip G., and Robert F. Dyer. 1976. "Brand Belief Measures in Deceptive Corrective Advertising: An Experimental Assessment." *Proceedings: 1976 Educator's Conference* 373–379.

Kuehl, Phillip G., and Robert F. Dyer. 1977. "Applications of the Normative Belief Technique for Measuring the Effectiveness of Deceptive and Corrective Advertisement." In *Advances in Consumer Research*, Vol. 4, edited by William Perreault, Jr., 204–212. Chicago: Association for Consumer Research.

Lavidge, Robert J. 1970. "The Growing Responsibilities of Marketing." *Journal of Marketing* 34 (January).

Lazer, William. 1969. "Marketing's Changing Social Relationships." *Journal of Marketing* 33 (January):3–9.

Lazer, William, and Eric H. Shaw. 1989. "Income, Assets and Consumption: The Relative Well Being of Mature Consumers." In *Quality-of-Life Studies in Marketing and Management*, edited by H. Lee Meadow and M. Joseph Sirgy, 265–279. Blacksburg, VA: Virginia Tech.

Levitt, Theodore. 1960. "Marketing Myopia." *Harvard Business Review* 38 (July–August).

Levitt, Theodore. 1975. "Marketing Myopia: Retrospective Commentary." *Harvard Business Review* 53 (September–October).

Loken, Barbara, Ivan Ross, and Ronald L. Hinkle. 1986. "Consumer 'Confusion' of Origin and Brand Similarity Perceptions." *Journal of Public Policy and Marketing* 5:195–211.

Lutz, Richard J. 1981. "The Role of Attitude Theory in Marketing." In *Perspectives in Consumer Behavior*, 3d ed., edited by Harold H. Kassarjian and Thomas S. Robertson. Glenview, IL: Scott, Foresman and Co.

Mentzer, John T., and A. Coskun Samli. 1981. "A Model for Marketing in Economic Development." *The Columbia Journal of World Business* (Fall):35–45.

Metzger, Robert O. 1989a. "The Banking Counterculture." *Bankers Monthly* (March):74.

Metzger, Robert O. 1989b. "Serving All the People All the Time." *Bank Marketing* (May):83.

Metzger, Robert O., and Sukhen, Dey. 1986. "Affluent Customers: What Do They Really Value?" *Journal of Retail Banking* (Fall):25–35.

Miller, James G. 1978. *Living Systems*. New York: McGraw-Hill.

Miller, Irwin. 1969. "Business Has a War to Win." *Harvard Business Review* 47 (March–April).

Monroe, Kent B. 1973. "Buyers' Subjective Perception of Price." *Journal of Marketing Research* 10:70–80.

Monroe, Kent B., and Susan M. Petroshius. 1981. "Buyers' Perception of Price: An Update of the Evidence." In *Perspectives in Consumer Behavior*, 3d ed., edited by Harold H. Kassarjian and Thomas S. Robertson. Glenview, IL: Scott, Foresman and Co.

Monti, Joseph. 1988. "Breaking the Doom Loop." *Mortgage Banking* (June):65–68.

Nader, Ralph. 1957. *Unsafe at Any Speed*. New York: Pocket Books.

Nader, Ralph. 1968. "The Great American Gyp." *The New York Review* (November 12).

Naisbitt, John. 1982. *Mega Trends*. New York: Warner Books.

Neustadt, David. 1988. "Calling Officers Win Praise; Turnover Troubles Firms." *American Banker Corporate Survey* 33–37.

Packard, Vance. 1957. *The Hidden Persuaders*. New York: Pocket Books.

Perry, M., and B. C. Hamm. 1969. "Canonical Analysis of Relations between Socio-Economic Risk and Personal Influence in Purchase Decisions." *Journal of Marketing Research* 6:352–358.

Peters, Tom, and Robert H. Waterman, Jr. 1982. *In Search of Excellence*. New York: Alfred A. Knopf.

Phillips, Kevin. 1991. *Politics of Rich and Poor*. New York: Harper Perennial.

Post, James E. 1990. "The Greening of Management." *Issues in Science and Technology* (Summer):68–72.

Reynolds, William H. 1971. *Products and Markets*. New York: Appleton-Century-Crofts.

"The Rich Are Richer—And America May Be the Poorer." 1991. *Business Week* (November 18):85–88.

Rogers, Everett M. 1976. "New Product Adoption and Diffusion." *Journal of Consumer Research* 290–301.

Ross, Ivan. 1974. "Perceived Risk and Consumer Behavior: A Critical Review." In *Advances in Consumer Research*, edited by M. J. Schlinger. Urbana, IL: Association for Consumer Research.

Samli, A. Coskun. 1969. "Differential Prices for the Rich and Poor." *University of Washington Business Review* (Summer):36–43.

Samli, A. Coskun. 1971. "Differential Price Indexes for the Negroes and Whites." *Mississippi Valley Business and Economic Review* (January).

Samli, A. Coskun. 1972. "De Facto Price Discrimination in the Food Purchaser of Rural Poor." *Journal of Retailing* (Fall):65–73.

Samli, A. Coskun. 1987. "Introduction." In *Marketing and the Quality-of-Life Interface*, edited by A. Coskun Samli, xv–xviii. New York: Quorum Books.

Samli, A. Coskun. 1989. *Retail Marketing Strategy*. New York: Quorum Books.

Samli, A. Coskun, and John M. Browning. 1991. "Exploring Modern American Wholesaling: An Assessment and Research Agenda." In *Developments in Marketing Science*, Vol. 14, edited by R. L. King, 86–90. Miami, FL: Academy of Marketing Science.

Samli, A. Coskun, Christian Palda, and Tansu Barker. 1987. "Toward a Mature Marketing Concept." *Sloan Management Review* (Winter):45–51.

Samli, A. Coskun, and M. Joseph Sirgy. 1982. "Social Responsibility in Marketing: An Analysis and Synthesis." In *Marketing Theory: A Philosophy of Science Perspective*, edited by R. F. Bush and S. D. Hunt, 250–254. Chicago: American Marketing Association.

Samli, A. Coskun, and M. Joseph Sirgy. 1981. "A Multi-Dimensional Approach to Analyzing Store Loyalty: A Predictive Model." In *The Changing Marketing Environment: New Theories and Applications*, edited by Ken Bernhardt and Bill Kehoe. Chicago: American Marketing Association.

Samuelson, Paul A. 1972. *Economics*, 9th ed. New York: McGraw-Hill Book Company.

Schiffman, Leon G. 1972. "Perceived Risk in New Product Trail by Elderly Consumers." *Journal of Marketing Research* 9:106–108.

Schiffman, Leon G., and Leslie L. Kanuk. 1990. *Consumer Behavior*. 3d ed. Englewood Cliffs, NJ: Prentice-Hall.

Sheshunoff, Alex. 1987. "Which Way the Bottom Line." *ABA Banking Journal* (August):33–36, 40.

Sheth, J. N., and M. Venkatesan. 1968. "Risk Reduction Processes in Repetitive Consumer Behavior." *Journal of Marketing Research* 5:307–310.

Sirgy, M. Joseph. 1985. "Using Self Congruity and Ideal Congruity to Predict Purchase Behavior." *Journal of Business Research* (June):195–206.

Streeter, William W. 1989. "Ready for the Challenge." *ABA Banking Journal* (October):95–98, 101.

Sturdivant, Frederick D. 1968. "Better Deal for Ghetto Shoppers." *Harvard Business Review* (March–April):130–139.

Sudo, Phillip T. 1988a. "Little Things Mean a Lot When It Comes to Service." *American Banker Corporate Survey* 23.

Sudo, Phillip T. 1988b. "Service Not Price is First Among Corporate Clients." *American Banker Corporate Survey* 15–18.

"Technology: Impact, The Mechanization of Retail Banking." 1983. *U.S. Banker* (June):71, 73.

Thorelli, Hans B. 1977. "Philosophies of Consumer Information Programs." In *Advances in Consumer Research*, Vol. 4, edited by W. D. Pereault, 282–287. Ann Arbor, MI: Association for Consumer Research.

Toffler, Alvin. 1990. *Power Shift*. New York: Bantam Books.

U.S. Environmental Protection Agency. 1988. *Office of Solid Waste and Emergency Response: Annual Report*. Washington, DC: U.S. Environmental Protection Agency, EPA/68-01-7259, November 1.

Violano, Michael. 1988. "Should Computers Answer Your Bank's Telephones." *Bankers Monthly* (July):38–42.

Walters, C. Glenn, and Blaise J. Bergiel. 1989. *Consumer Behavior*. Cincinnati: South-Western Publishing Co.

"What We're Hearing About Voice Response." 1987. *ABA Banking Journal* (May):74, 76.

Wright, Peter. 1975. "Consumer Choice Strategies: Simplifying versus Optimizing." *Journal of Marketing Research* 12:60–67.

Young, Lawrence E. 1990. "Ads Targeting Blacks Become Blacks' Target." *Dallas Morning News* (May 20), section B, page 12.

Zeithaml, Valerie A. 1981. "How Consumer Evaluation Processes Differ between Goods and Services." In *Marketing of Services*, edited by J. H. Donnelly and William R. George. Chicago: American Marketing Association.

Index

ABOUT THE AUTHOR

A. COSKUN SAMLI is a Research Professor of Marketing and International Business at the University of North Florida at Jacksonville. His most recent books include *Retail Marketing Strategies, Marketing and the Quality-of-Life Interface,* and *Technology Transfer* (Quorum 1989, 1987, 1985). He is the author or co-author of more than thirty other booklength studies and over two hundred articles in the field of marketing. Dr. Samli was a Ford Foundation Fellow, Sears AACSB Fellow, Fulbright Distinguished Lecturer, and AACSB Beta Gamma Sigma L. J. Buchan Distinguished Professor. He has done numerous projects on poverty, the elderly, and the quality of life.